TRUE PATH
of the NINJA

TRUE PATH *of the* NINJA

THE DEFINITIVE TRANSLATION OF THE *SHONINKI*

ANTONY CUMMINS
YOSHIE MINAMI

Foreword by OTAKE RISUKE

Preface by Dr. NAKASHIMA ATSUMI

TUTTLE Publishing

Tokyo | Rutland, Vermont | Singapore

Please note that the publisher and author(s) of this instructional book are NOT RESPON-SIBLE in any manner whatsoever for any injury that may result from practicing the techniques and/or following the instructions given within. Martial arts training can be dangerous—both to you and to others—if not practiced safely. If you're in doubt as to how to proceed or whether your practice is safe, consult with a trained martial arts teacher before beginning. Since the physical activities described herein may be too strenuous in nature for some read-ers, it is also essential that a physician be consulted prior to training.

Published by Tuttle Publishing, an imprint of Periplus Editions (HK) Ltd.

www.tuttlepublishing.com

Library of Congress cataloging in process.

ISBN 978-4-8053-1439-5

Distributed by

North America, Latin America & Europe
Tuttle Publishing
364 Innovation Drive
North Clarendon, VT 05759-9436 U.S.A.
Tel: (802) 773-8930
Fax: (802) 773-6993
info@tuttlepublishing.com
www.tuttlepublishing.com

Japan
Tuttle Publishing
Yaekari Building, 3rd Floor
5-4-12 Osaki, Shinagawa-ku
Tokyo 141 0032
Tel: (81) 3 5437-0171
Fax: (81) 3 5437-0755
sales@tuttle.co.jp
www.tuttle.co.jp

Second edition
24 23 22 21   5 4 3   2112VP

Printed in Malaysia

This book is dedicated to

John Cummins

My father, who has fueled this entire venture

ACKNOWLEDGMENTS

A special thank you to Dr. Nakashima,
for without his solid work on the *Shoninki* manual
this project would not have been possible. Also to Mr. Otake,
the head of the Katori school, who was a true gentleman.

Contents

PART THREE

The Shoninki Middle Chapters . . 95

PART FOUR

The Shoninki Final Chapters . . 145

---

* These chapters were not featured in the original table of contents and one
presumes that the author simply missed including them. Therefore, they have been
added here for the ease of the modern reader.

Foreword

It was totally unexpected that I would be asked to write the foreword for this publication of the ninjutsu densho, *True Path of the Ninja* (or the *Shoninki*) by Mr. Antony Cummins and Ms. Yoshie Minami, but I take pleasure in writing a few words for this book.

In Japan, ninjutsu, or the shinobi, has been well known and has been on everyone's lips since old times. However, the truth about ninjutsu is what you cannot see, say or hear, thus *see no evil, speak no evil and hear no evil.* Therefore, ninjutsu would only be handed down as the most secret of secrets and only from a special person to another special one. Though people in the modern world perceive ninjutsu as nothing more than that which is found within the pages of comics or novels, the true art of ninjutsu and the ninja are what we might call spies, which are still active today.

True Path of the Ninja, which has been published here in the English language, in my opinion, is the most excellent masterpiece of all the manuscripts on ninjutsu that have ever been written. Also, knowledge, even if it is out of use now, is something you

never get too much of. If you read this book,
I am certain that there should be something
here that you may find helpful in the course
of your life.

— Otake Risuke
Katori Shinto-Ryu, Head Teaching Master

Teachings from the Ninja for Our Modern Society

First of all I would like to express my sincere respect and gratitude to Antony Cummins and Yoshie Minami for their work on this translation of the *Shoninki*, the secret account of ninjutsu, for Tuttle Publishing, who made the decision to record this notable feat.

Seen in its true perspective, 忍術 means "to be physically and mentally tough and prepared to carry out secret plans at all costs" and 術 means "measures to achieve your aim." Thus, 忍者 (ninja) can be defined as "those who have learned the skills to survive, to choose a proper objective and to achieve it by making a steady effort in training in ninjutsu." If you read the *Shoninki* again and again, you will notice that ninja were masters of all kinds of living skills, and that this book not only tells you about conspiracy, destruction, and killing, but also offers instruction for every aspect of your life and provides help during any circumstance.

The absolute goal for a ninja was success and survival. In the late Warring Period in Japan, when Oda Nobunaga, the strongest warlord at that time, was conducting his successful campaign across the country, the ninja faced his fearful power with courage even though they were insignificant in comparison to Nobunaga. They once managed to repel his son's army but ended up being wiped out by his massive cleanup operation. However, it turned out that they didn't die out but came back to life in the next stage of history.

When we look at modern society, it seems that market mechanisms and global standards are our new rules for living. These American-style standards, backed by their strong financial and military capabilities, have a tendency to equalize the world and minimize the individuality of countries. While it is desirable for everybody in every country to share common sense and morals, the result of pursuing market principles is that the concentration of wealth is being put into the hands of the few while increasing the number of those living in poverty. From a broader point of view, we are always living in a "warring period."

Because of the modern world's similarities with the Warring Period, we can learn various things from the ninja who survived those times. Although they did not enjoy any measure of social privilege, they were neither winners nor losers during this tumultuous time. This noteworthy accomplishment provides us with teachings and insights into life. To live with spiritual richness within modern society where a gap between the rich and the poor is ever widening, you need to change your sense of value and be confident in yourself.

Here are three essential requirements to be a ninja:
1. **To always think outside of the box.** Any kind of boundaries, such as commonplace assumptions, as well as physical barriers in daily life are things the ninja needs to circumvent. A ninja can do anything as long as it is in accordance with their own sense of value and the justice of the group they belong to, even if it is seen as bad from the viewpoint of socially accepted norms.
2. **To be affiliated with some kind of organization.** It was often

the case that ninja were given allowances by a daimyo or the Court to work under their direction, so when they went on a mission, their expenses were covered by their employers.

3. **What ninjas did was meant to benefit their employers.** They sometimes did dirty jobs such as assassinations, theft, or robbery, but these all must be done for the benefit of their employer. If they used ninjutsu for their own interest, it would be mere theft and robbery. For fear of this, most secret manuscripts teach that a ninja should be always right-minded. If the ninja were merely thieves, no one would hire them.

Besides the practical skills of infiltration, making gunpowder, signaling, field medicine and so on, ninjutsu includes a vast range of spiritual techniques such as Shugendo religious mountain worship (a mixture of Shinto, Buddhism and shamanistic beliefs using Zen, spells, etc.) through which they intended to enhance their abilities by developing self-control. On top of that, they had a unique close-knit community developed over generations, so they helped each other as the occasion arose even if they were working for opposite sides.

They were also characterized by a limited amount of activity expense, inventing tools on their own, being hired by outside bodies on a temporary basis, having an ordinary job and so on.

The most distinctive feature of all is that they had mastery of skills that affected every aspect of life. It was in the sixteenth century, the turbulent age of the Warring Period, when ninjutsu attained its most drastic development. At that time they didn't live like the secret service in the castle or in "Sherwood Forest" but they lived in town as ordinary people. To a layman's eyes they looked like a peasant, hairdresser, monkey trainer, merchant, etc. Beneath the surface they were part of an underworld society of ninja, bonded by an oath made between each other. This discreet shadow existence of ninjas once confronted powerful authority, then strengthened their power, and then eventually disappeared into thin air with the shifting winds of the times.

This *True Path of the Ninja* is written in a pragmatic way, but it is not easy to understand its underlying meaning. To have a deeper insight into the author's intentions, you have to read between the lines. Whether you can reach a true understanding or not greatly depends on your own experience, your questioning mind, and your age. As you grow older, every time you reread this book you will obtain a new perspective. I hope this book will be an enjoyable and awakening experience for you every time you read it.

— *Dr. Nakashima Atsumi*

INTRODUCTION

The Shoninki

Lay before you in these pages are the deepest secrets of the ninja. The ancient scroll translated here is the *Shoninki* (正忍記)—a true shinobi account and one of three ninja scrolls from a samurai warfare school known as Natori-Ryu (名取流). The term *shinobi* or *shinobi no mono* is the correct way of saying ninja in medieval Japanese. The scroll was written by the samurai Natori Sanjuro Masazumi (名取三十郎正澄), who was known to his peers as Issui Sensei and was a warrior who served Lord Tokugawa Yorinobu as a close retainer and warfare specialist in the city of Wakayama, Japan. The *Shoninki* is only one of approximately 30 manuals that make up the Natori School of samurai warfare, and is the final ninja scroll of the whole curriculum. A student of Natori-Ryu is expected to have studied the main scrolls before they arrive at the secret teachings of the shinobi, thus the *Shoninki* is written from the perspective that the student has a full knowledge of samurai warfare and the details of Natori-Ryu. Therefore, as a modern reader, understand that while this manual may seem vague in parts or lacking in specifics, it was written for warriors who could fill in the gaps though years of mastery in samurai ways. Therefore this scroll

正忍記序

支爲忍兵之術也其来尚矣眞ニ
謀策之捄航軍師之關鍵而進ニ
退利審取撃柔也爲ル士之者悪得
而忽諸爲其事也渉累卵之
危凌倒懸之急不至難哉臨ニ

The first page of the Shoninki *from the transcription in the National Diet Library*

should be seen as a final "conversation" between Natori Masa-zumi himself and his students, giving them a full understand-ing of the ways of the ninja.

The *Shoninki* was written in 1681 and was kept as a secret

document available only to the most ardent students—it was not meant for public dissemination and it was not until the early twentieth century that it was first published, at which point it formed the foundation for Japanese research into the lost identity of the shinobi warrior. Over the past century it has been hailed as one of, if not the finest examples of shinobi literature, because unlike the majority of ninja scrolls, it is fully explicit on the teachings. It does not aim to hide anything, nor is it simply a memorandum list—a common trait of shinobi manuals. Furthermore, it is considered as *kuden* (the full oral tradition) for the manuals that precede it, that is the scrolls named: *Shinobi no Maki* and *Dakko Shinobi no Maki*, all three together create the Natori-Ryu ninja arts. The original *Shoninki* is currently missing and only a few transcriptions exist. In the main, most people are aware of and use the Natori Hyozaemon transcription of 1743, which can be found in the Japanese National Diet Library (catalogue number: 214–9).

The shinobi of Japan are a worldwide icon, a household name and one of Japan's most popular cultural assets, and the *Shoninki* is one of the premier representations of the historical ninja. The manual is deceptively deep and written so that with each reading, more lessons are found, and avenues that you did not see before open up. Thus, treasure this collection of ancient teachings and enjoy your journey into the world of the infamous ninja.

The Arts of the Ninja

The arts of the ninja are collectively known to the modern world as "ninjutsu" (忍術), but they should correctly be termed "*shinobi no jutsu*" (忍の術)—literally, "shinobi skills." Shinobi no jutsu itself is not a complete system for a warrior; instead, it is an auxiliary art, a skill set that is attached to a warrior's military training. Samurai and *ashigaru* (foot soldiers) would be trained in multiple aspects of warfare, including some or all of the following; armor and equipment, weapons handling, unarmed combat, horse riding, formations, troop maneuvres, military tactics, warfare skills, esoteric rituals, encampment rules, scouting, incendiary training and Chinese military classics, among others. It was here that a very select few—some of which came from the same families—would also study shinobi no jutsu, which can be considered as "black ops" and spying. It was through this speciality that the ninja were born.

Shinobi no mono were hired by a lord to act as covert agents and would accompany an army, or infiltrate a target enemy months or years before a campaign was initiated. In Japan's Warring Period of the fifteenth and sixteenth century, the arts of the ninja were performed by warriors and soldiers of different social standing, meaning that many of the ninja agents were of the samurai class and an unknown percentage were foot soldiers. The position of ninja itself crossed social boundaries. From highly sophisticated and intellectual samurai who had to deal with high end intelligence gathering and operations to low level infiltration commandos, both of whom worked in unison to deceive and disrupt the strength of the enemy. The concept of ninja as a secret underclass or a collection of peasant families against the ruling samurai is a modern myth, and many ninja documents are written by the samurai, and therefore, ninjutsu is a samurai art and is a vital part of the Japanese military machine.

Natori Masazumi himself says that the ways of the ninja are hard to define and that such skills are like a void, there are no edges or boundaries in its description and that no clear line defines that which is a ninja skill and that which is not. Therefore, to understand the subject, consider that ninjutsu is in essence the intention to deceive the enemy or to engage in covert operations. Ninjutsu borrows from other areas; a grappling hook is by no means only used by the ninja, but when used to scale a castle wall by a single operative or small group, it becomes ninjutsu. Likewise, when performing arson, the concept of *kajutsu* (火術)—fire skills—comes into the realm of ninjutsu. However, the presence of deception does not always equate to ninjutsu; hiding a troop formation or an ambush is not ninjutsu—they are simply military deceptions, and so the lines become blurred on what is, and what is not classed as a shinobi skill. On the whole, a single operative or small group of operatives who actively devote themselves to the deception, infiltration and disruption of the enemy by using techniques which are collectively recorded by the ninja of history can be said to be performing shinobi no jutsu—the skills of the shinobi.

Shinobi no jutsu pertains to skills in the following areas:

- Infiltrating enemy camps, castles, compounds or houses
- Tools used for infiltration
- Spying and intelligence missions
- Battle camp defense responsibilities
- Night patrols
- The discovery of enemy shinobi attempting to infiltrate a camp or castle
- The discovery of enemy shinobi who are in disguise
- Disguise and impersonation
- Counterintelligence systems
- Methods of propaganda
- Close and deep scouting
- Enemy troop observation
- Arson and explosives
- Poisons and powders
- Esoteric magic
- Criminal capture missions
- The discovery of rebellions and plots, both internal and external

All of the above create a network of skills, some borrowed and some specific to the ninja, but all of which represent an auxiliary art used by specific agents known to us as the ninja. For a more detailed understanding of the shinobi see; *In Search of the Ninja* (The History Press).

Natori-Ryu

Natori-Ryu is the school of *gungaku* (軍学): military studies of the Natori family. It originated in the second half of the sixteenth

century when the Natori clan served the famed warlord Takeda
Shingen. The original founder is recorded as Natori Yoichinojo
Masatoshi, who was a samurai in the vanguard of Takeda's army.
Initially, the school focused on military strategy and also formed
a medical unit, being famous for their secret technique to cure
sword wounds. After the defeat of the Takeda clan by the

NATORI RYU

TOKUGAWA YORINOBU
LORD OF KISHU DOMAIN

Tokugawa family, the retainers of Takeda Shingen—Natori included—signed oaths to join and fight for the Tokugawa Clan. From here the Natori split up into two main branches, the Edo-Natori line and the Kishu-Natori line.

The Tokugawa Family can be divided into four branches, the main line of the Shogun in Edo (modern day Tokyo) and the three great house of the Tokugawa family (*gosanke*) which was made up of the House of Owari, The House of Kii (Kishu) and the House of Mito. The former is the seat of the Shogun while the latter three are the lines in place when a male heir is not available from the main line.

Sometime in the first half of the seventeenth century, Natori Sanjuro Masazumi was born into the Kishu-Natori line, the fourth son of Natori Yajiemon Masatoyo. Natori Masazumi— the author of the *Shoninki*—was to become the *chuko no so* for Natori-Ryu, meaning "grandmaster of redefinition," as it was this Natori member who became the core grandmaster of the school. He studied Kusunoki-Ryu from the lineage of Kusunoki Fuden, and along with other schools such as Koshu-Ryu, he greatly expanded the scope of Natori-Ryu and recorded the school's vast teachings in a collection of scrolls, the *Shoninki* being one of many. The school curriculum was expansive and reached into all areas of Japanese warfare, from those skills needed to be a samurai of the day to Chinese formations, from the various positions within an army and their given tasks to esoteric cosmology, from weapon and tool terminology and use to the philosophy of the mind and of course, the arts of the shinobi among many, many others.

Sometime in the seventeenth century—according to the Natori Family traditions—Lord Tokugawa Yorinobu instructed Natori Masazumi that he should change the school name from Natori-Ryu to Shin-Kusunoki-Ryu, meaning the new school of Kusunoki. Due to this, various Natori manuals are labeled as both Kusunoki-Ryu and Shin-Kusunoki-Ryu. The general rule of thumb is that anything Natori-Ryu or Shin-Kusunoki-Ryu is the writing of Natori Masazumi, while Kusunoki-Ryu proper have multiple different branches. The original name of Natori-Ryu has been readopted for two reasons; firstly to avoid confusion, and secondly because official Tokugawa Clan records show the school recorded as Natori-Ryu by the nineteenth century.

The school continued in the form Natori Masazumi created until its closure with the Meiji Restoration. The school passed from the Natori family into other hands and back to the Natori family only to be passed on again during its career.

Natori-Ryu Grandmasters

The following is a current list of the Natori-Ryu grandmasters, this list was compiled from records in the Wakayama Prefectural Library in Wakayama city.

1. Natori Yoichinojo Masatoshi (founder)
2. Natori Yajiemon Masatoyo
3. Natori Sanjuro Masazumi (grandmaster of redefinition)
4. Natori Hyozaemon Kuninori
5. Natori (Unobe) Matasaburo (adopted and given twenty koku salary)
6. Ohata Kihachiro (passed it back to the Natori family)
7. Natori Kusujuro
8. Yabutani Yoichi
9. Tomiyama Umon
10. Yabutani Yoichiro

With the close of the samurai age and the Meiji Restoration, the final grandmaster, Yabutani Yoichiro, closed the school due to the modernization of Japan. The old ways of war were being superseded by the modern military. While the main branch closed, at least one line of Natori-Ryu continued to exist on the island of Shikoku, but in the twentieth century that too closed down, making Natori-Ryu an extinct school.

Antony Cummins with Yabutani Itaru, the grandson of the last Natori-Ryu grandmaster

A Biography of Natori Sanjuro Masazumi

The Japanese family crest used by Natori Sanjuro Masazumi

Natori Sanjuro Masazumi was born at some point in the first half of the seventeenth century and was most likely a child of the first or second generation after the great wars. Hence, most older people around him were veterans of the great wars of Japan and that Natori would have been surrounded by battle-tested elders and the sons of those who directly fought in the wars. It is known that his elder brother, Natori Yajiemon Masakatsu, was a retainer to Lord Tokugawa Yorinobu, and that in 1654 Natori Masazumi himself was brought to service as a *chukosho*—a form squire. Natori appears to have closely served the Tokugawa family for life, holding the following positions:

- *chukosho* — squire-page
- *goshoinban* — warrior in service in the castle
- *gokinjuzume* — close retainer to the lord
- *ogoban* — military officer
- *daikosho* — personal attendant to the lord

This means that Natori's life would have been one of a castle samurai, serving his duties around the Kishu branch of the Tokugawa family, tending to the Lord's needs and requirements and ensuring his safety as one of his personal guard. When Lord Tokugawa Yorinobu retired Natori Masazumi continued to serve him at his residence until the lord's death. Outside of those services, he was a dedicated student of war and clearly worried for the future of samurai skills. In his writings he hints that the samurai of his time are starting to forget the old ways of battle and that a new era of peaceful samurai with no experience are rising. For this reason he devoted himself to studying and collecting the secrets of the old ways which are dying around him, and to record them for prosperity. From his teachings he produced a collection of writings that survive to this day:

- A ten volume collection of *gungaku* military studies manuals
- A single volume containing eighteen short scrolls on warfare
- Three scrolls dedicated to the arts of the shinobi
- A twelve volume encyclopedia of samurai equipment and ways
- Nine inherited scrolls of deeper secrets
- A manual on the eight formations of an army

His collected works are vast and expansive, crossing all realms of samurai life. The *Shoninki* is only a single work, having its own place within the full catalogue of Natori-Ryu.

In 1685 Natori Masazumi retired to the village of Ono at the foot of Mt. Koya—the holy mountain of the Shingon faith—where it is presumed he taught his grandson, Natori Hyozaemon, the ways of Natori-Ryu after the death of his own son. Natori Masazumi—or Issui sensei as he is known to others—died at an unknown age on the 5th of May, 1708. His death certificate and grave can be seen on pages 103 and 104. His nom de plume was Toissui (藤一水), and his Buddhist death name was Kyugenin Tekigan Ryosuikoji (窮源院滴岩了水居士). His remains were interred at Eunji Temple (恵運寺) in the city of Wakayama. His grave can be seen today, and all visitors are welcome.

Eunji Temple
Eunji Temple is the home of one branch of the decedents of the famous warrior Yamamoto Kansuke, and it remains under the care of the Yamamoto Family with the current keeper, Yamamoto Jyuho.

The temple appears to have been a place of worship of decedents for those samurai who served Takeda Shingen and who had moved to Kishu together. The Kishu-Natori branch are interred here, from the beginning of their move to Wakayama up until today. The last male member of the Natori Clan to bear the name Natori was Natori Tetsuo who died in 1949 with no children. His brother, Natori Takao, had already adopted the different surname of Kano and could not return to Natori after the death of his brother. Therefore, the last Natori was Natori Yukiko, but being female, her name changed when she married into the Ishigaki family and she died in 1995. The Natori Clan graves are now under the care of her children—the last true descendants to be born from a named Natori member.

Monk Yamamoto and the temple take a proactive approach to the *Shoninki* and the skills of Natori-Ryu. The monk has formed a reading study group called "Shoninki wo Yomu Kai" (正忍記を

Monk Yamamoto Jyuho—gravekeeper to the Natori Family

読む会) and hold events and workshops on the study of the text and the promotion of Wakayama. Again, readers are welcome to visit the temple.

The Translation

The *Shoninki* is unlike other ninja manuals. Many shinobi scrolls are simply memorandum lists where the original skill is not described and only a guess can be made regarding its specifics. Others have vast detail, explaining the ways of the shinobi in all aspects, but they are simple in their instruction, and their translation is relatively easy with the only real difficulty being lost vocabulary or poor transcriptions. The *Shoninki* stands alone from the others because of its style. It assumes that the reader has read and been trained in the ways of all the other Natori scrolls, and therefore a sentence in the *Shoninki* can be loaded with stacks of required background reading, experience and cultural knowledge. Furthermore, many of the sentences are subjective, other manuals tend to be firmly objective—"do X, move to Y and carry out Z"—but the *Shoninki* is built on a foundation where such instructional learning has previously been achieved by the student and moves into the realm of a "conversation," where meaning can be interpreted by the reader. This is clear when read alongside the scroll *Dakko Shinobi no Maki* as the *Shoninki* is clearly an extension of that. While the majority of the text is identifiable between different translations, there are aspects where interpretation is required, and no matter who the translator is, personal opinion on meaning has to take place. Our team holds the special position of being the only team to have used the collection of the Natori scrolls to validate our translation of the text and therefore this translation is the only one supported by actual Natori teachings. That being said, at the request of the publisher we took the original translation and spliced the footnotes in for an easier read and also removed all macron markings (ō & ū). Thus, in this version, added information from our background reading is included in the text to ensure a smoother experience for the reader. When reading this version, understand that some of the supplementary information is a combination of information from the other Natori scrolls, academic research and grammatical points to give flow. No matter who translates this text, each person has to step into the realm of interpretation due to its very nature. Of all the manuals left to the world, the *Shoninki* is the most enigmatic.

It is my pleasure to introduce the second edition of this translation. We have attempted to correct any clear mistakes we made in the first edition and to bring into focus any aspects that were too obscure in our first version. For any differences in text, this edition takes precedence. Since its first publication, our understanding of Natori and his works has grown exponentially, and we can now minimize those areas of subjective interpretation, bringing us closer to Natori Masazumi's original vision.

Natori-Ryu Reborn

The final days of Natori-Ryu were played out in the twentieth century as the last known branch closed its doors, and the manuals were placed on shelves to wait for a new surge of life. The wonderful aspect of Natori-Ryu is that the scrolls are filled with detail, the prime example being the *Shoninki*. The other Natori-Ryu scrolls possess equally detailed information, each one working together to form a collective set of teachings. In the instances where the text is vague, fortune has provided multiple transcriptions, each one with additional commentaries. These commentaries are the oral traditions which accompany the scrolls but which were written down at a later stage, providing the hidden details and leaving only a very few unanswered questions. Such favorable circumstances has left a window for the school to be resurrected and re-established as one of the premier war schools of samurai arts.

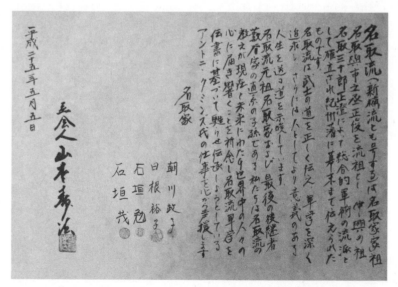

The blessing given by the Natori Family on the 5th of May, 2013

On May 5th, 2013, the remaining Natori Family members in the presence of Monk Yamamoto at Eunji Temple gave their blessings for Natori-Ryu to be resurrected under my guidance. With the support of both the Natori Family and the temple, the school has enjoyed a successful rebirth and is currently active.

Alongside this volume of the Shoninki, *Natori-Ryu's teachings are also given in full in* The Book of Samurai *series*

The resurrected Natori-Ryu is comprised of groups who dedicate themselves to the teachings of Natori Masazumi and who communicate with other members around the world. The school is active on most social media platforms and we encourage people to get involved with the school's ancient teachings. All members come together in the spirit of research and development with the aim to help one another understand the benefits of old Japanese ways. Currently the focal point for all students of Natori is the Facebook group "Natori Ryu Hub," and I invite you to explore and discover our school. Further information can be found at our website: www.natori.co.uk. All that remains is to encourage you to study this manual instead of simply reading it, and enjoy these teachings while you find a place for the principles within your lives.

—*Antony Cummins*

PART ONE

The Preface to the Shoninki

正忍記 序
Shoninki Jo

This introduction to the Shoninki *sets the foundation for what a shinobi is in the minds of the ninja themselves. Natori takes you through what it means to train as a ninja and what it means to live your life by the ways of the shinobi.*

Having worked in secret on this covert book, Natori visited a high-ranking samurai of his clan late in the night, asking for words to accompany the secret arts of the ninja, arts that would be handed down from father to son. Katsuda Kakyusai Yoshin was the name of this samurai—a warrior we know nothing about. He did as Natori asked and wrote a preface for this shinobi text. This preface gives us a great insight into what the samurai thought of those who trained as ninjas. Even back then, in feudal Japan, we can see that the samurai believed that a ninja could disappear into the black of the night, becoming "invisible"—a testament to the skills of stealth accredited to the legendary ninja.

It has been many years since the basis for the arts of the shinobi soldiers were developed and brought into existence. The arts of the shinobi soldier are a rudder in the planning of a strategy and the key to success for all tacticians. Also, the shinobi have vital information on whether to advance or retreat and the advantages and disadvantages of a given situation. Could any warrior neglect or disregard this?

The art of the ninja deals with the most perilous situations and instructs on how to survive the most agonizing of endeavors. When being challenged at night by a night patrol and the shinobi is not a very capable one, if he cannot manage a situation in a tactful and eloquent way; if he cannot do it without feeling any sense of panic; if he is weak—he will not be able to achieve his goal of deception. If you entrust the wrong person with a critical task, the result will be disastrous, almost as if you had given your men to the enemy, or given a thief your food and rations. Therefore, you should select the best recruits for ninjutsu training and give them discipline.

Lately, Toissui Masatake has recorded this secret document on the art of the *ninpei* by his own hand. The esoteric way of this writing is extremely scrupulous and subtle. If you attentively trust in and perform these ninjutsu skills, there wouldn't be a single warrior you couldn't deceive, no matter how prudent and discreet he was. Doubtlessly you would be able to take hold of the enemy by your tactics and have complete control over them. You can do this by having them "eat out of the palm of your hand" at will. It seems almost magical, this art of night stealth that enables you to make yourself invisible in the black of night.

One day, after he finished the manual, he brought it to me discreetly and asked me to write a preface for it. As I am not on the same path as he is and thus, lacking in good judgment to be able to fulfill this request, I tried to turn it down, but he didn't allow me to refuse. Therefore, I am obliged hereby to provide these words and to preface this document, though it seems redundant because of my lack of understanding.

延宝九年　初秋哉生明

The year of 1681 (Enpo 9), the 3rd day of the lunar calendar in early autumn

紀城散人　勝田何求斎養真
之を書す

Written by Katsuda Kakyusai Yoshin, Warrior* of the Kishu Domain

---

* Literally, "freeman." The kanji used in this name was also used to denote an artist."

Summary of the Tradition

當流正忍記

Toryu Shoninki

Natori opens his book with his understanding of the history of the shinobi. He discusses how they came to be established and how their arts moved around Japan, allowing us to understand how he came to be given the skills of a master ninja. Here, he demonstrates solidarity between shinobi clans and a rare glimpse into how they banded together. Secrets were shared between people who did not know each other but who could prove themselves to be worthy of the title: ninja. This value of harmony is something that we could learn from in our world today; a harmony built on a trust and respect given to people who walk the same path, no matter the origin of their skills.

Shinobi have existed in Japan since ancient times but their existence was highlighted at these following points: the Genpei War 源平合戦 of 1180–1185, a conflict that took place between the Heike and Genji 源氏 clans that resulted in the Heike clan's defeat and the establishment of the Kamakura shogunate, when Minamoto no Kuro Yoshitsune 源九郎義経* picked up and used brave men like Ise no Saburo Yoshimori 伊勢三郎義盛,† and also in the Kemmu 建武 Period of 1334–1336, Kusunoki Masashige 楠木正成‡ used shinobi several times.

---

* Yoshitsune (1159–1189), a general of the Genji clan and a younger brother of Minamoto no Yoritomo, the founder of the Kamakura shogunate. He reputedly was taught the martial arts by a *shugenja* 修験者, that is a *shugendo* 修験道 practitioner or more famously known as the *Yamabushi* mountain priests. Yoshitsune spent his childhood in a monastery where he acquired a copy of the *Rikutou* 六韜—the *Six Secret Teachings*, which was one of ancient China's Seven Military Classics. *Shugenja* or *Yamabushi* 山伏 lived in esoteric practice in the mountains and it is widely understood that there is a definite connection between ninjutsu and *shugendo*, a religion with roots in animism, which later included Shinto and Buddhism. It has been postulated that En-no-gyoja 役行者, the founder of *shugendo*, was the originator of ninjutsu—a statement without foundation.

† This appears to be a reference to Ise no Saburo Yoshimori 伊勢三郎義盛 (?–1186), one of Yoshitsune's four major retainers. He appears in various writings and there are several different versions about where he originated. It is understood that he was born in Iga and was said to have been a brigand in the mountains of Suzuka, leading hundreds of men when he attacked Yoshitsune's army and was defeated. Yoshitsune used Ise no Saburo Yoshimori and his men and it is this union that the author is alluding to when he says "brave men." Furthermore, Yoshimori's name is used in the title of the document, *Yoshimori Hyakushu* よしもり百首—*Yoshimori's 100 Verses*. It includes 100 verses for the shinobi or *shinobiuta*. They were constructed of 31 syllables each and teach the secrets of ninjutsu. Fourteen of them are referred to in the *Bansenshukai* 萬川集海. As these were collected more than 500 years after Yoshimori's death, it is doubtful that he himself wrote those verses, but it is presumed that they used his name, as he was considered an ancestor of the shinobi.

‡ Kusunoki Masashige (1294–1336) was a warrior well known for his loyalty to the Emperor Godaigo and his outstanding tactics in battles. He was a leader of a certain *akuto* 悪党 group (literally, "evil bands"), some of which became effective at disturbing the political peace of the time. Masashige was possibly a captain of a powerful *akuto* group that was practicing predation with hundreds of people from Iga. Although it cannot be said he himself was a ninja, his skillful arts of war gave birth to or influenced ninjutsu later on. It is possible that the foundation for shinobi organizations came from these *akuto* in the medieval times.

A number of generations later, Hojo Ujiyasu 北条氏康* employed a thief or *nusubito* 盗人 called Kazama 風麻† by giving him land-rights called *chigyo* 知行 and sent him and his retinue out to various places and provinces to investigate the situation. Shingen 信玄 of Koshu 甲州‡ employed those called *suppa*, who were also thieves of the Kai province.

Later, the people from Koka 甲賀, next to Iga 伊賀, followed this path of ninjutsu, and having made the oath of *Ichigun Ichimi* 一郡一味, the friendship oath of "one district and one band," joining the people together. They went out expansively to various provinces to use their skills. Thus, being universally recognized as the premier shinobi, they exchanged a firm written form of oath, which says "If I come to where you are, you should show me everything of your province, and if you come to where I am, I will show you everything about my province." By doing this, it is said they should show that their family tradition was extraordinarily exquisite and outstanding and also show the marvel of their tradition of ninjutsu, at its best. However, being asked what they should do regarding the offspring of shinobi, or if a complete

---

* Born in 1515 and dying in 1571, Hojo Ujitsuna was the third warlord of the Odawara Hojo 小田原北条 clan. Hojo Ujitsuna's 北条氏綱 son fought against Uesugi Kenshin 上杉謙信 and Takeda Shingen 武田信玄 to rule as far as south Kozuke 上野. As both a gifted general and administrator, he stands out as one of the foremost rulers of his day.

† Kazama 風麻 refers to Fuma Kotaro 風魔小太郎 (?–1603?). Fuma is an alternative way of reading the Japanese ideogram for Kazama as he was born in the Kazama region of the Sagami province. According to *Hojo Godaiki* 北条五代記, the journal of the five generations of the Hojo clan, he was seven feet tall and led a band of 200 people. The record says they were called *Rappa* 乱波, professionals in night attacks and infiltration and also good at deception. They were divided into four subgroups of pirates, mountain brigands, burglars, and robbers. However, it appears that they may have been more like mercenaries than shinobi.

‡ Takeda Shingen (1521–1573), the eldest son of Takeda Nobutora 武田信虎, leader of the Takeda clan and the daimyo of the Kai province. It is commonly known that he employed 70 Koshu *suppa*. He selected the top 30 candidates, took their wives and children under his custody, put them under oath, and entrusted ten of them to each of three retainers. Later, he made up an organization of 200 *suppa* by recruiting widely from monks, merchants, and peasants as well as *Bushi*. They were called *Mitsumono* 三ツ者, and were in charge of espionage, deception, and counterespionage. He was called Ashinagabozu 足長坊主, "the long-legged monk," a reference to how he used shinobi freely and expansively while "moving around quickly."

stranger comes along without recognition, there is a traditional way of constructing a torch within the clan. You should regard this torch as evidence, so that you should never suspect anyone who bears it.

Other than these examples, some experts in robbery have written down their achievements and claimed that it is a family tradition to be handed down for generations. Nowadays, these so called schools or *ryugi* of the shinobi, which are widespread in the world, are simply schools for thieves. But we are not thieves; this account is of our school.

The Types of Shinobi Soldiers

忍兵之品

Ninpei no Shina

We think of the ninja as a solitary agent, but this is not true. While they are all collectively known as shinobi, there are multiple variations on this theme. Natori shows us that each version of the ninja, and those who are not ninja but are on the periphery, have different responsibilities, helping support the "field ninja" in their mission. Additionally, he shows us the negative side of people with these skills; they were thieves and blackguards, who used their skills for personal gain and egotistical reasons. We, as people of the martial way, can understand this in today's world of capitalism and its culture. We can learn from Natori the valuable lessons found in unification and understanding our skills. We can also learn how to use them for the collective good, avoiding the path of destruction and decay.

The Skills of Espionage

Tokan 唐間	The Spies of China or *Gokan* 五間
	The Five types of spies
Kyodo 郷導	How to be guided by locals
Togiki 外聞	Hearing information from the outside
Ninja 忍者	The "Stealers in"
Nusubito 盗人	"Thieves and scum"

A man, who knows everything of ninjutsu and takes ownership of what he has learned, while at the same time always keeping it in mind and conducting himself independently, is called a shinobi. When two or three people conduct ninjutsu mutually, they are called *so-nin* 双忍 or "twin-ninjas." When this is the case, you should be aware that unless both or all of them are competent, they will not work well together and the goal at hand will not be attained. In ancient times, it was considered difficult to work with too many people in a group. It is said that there were many courageous masters in the past, but all of their achievements were accomplished independently. The young and unworthy people of today are in no way equal to their ancient counterparts—how could they work well in teams of twos or threes? They simply would not be successful. Thus, it must be said that ninjutsu is the highest form of intelligence within the army.

Tokan

The *Tokan* Chinese spies were first identified during the reign of Huang-di 黄帝, the legendary Yellow Emperor of China, whose personal name is pronounced "Nokizaru" in Japanese. A name which interestingly also became another name for the shinobi used in the Uesugi clan of Echigo.

In the chronicle of Zuo Zhuan 左伝, these Chinese spies were called *cho* 長. Later, they were also called *saisaku* さい作 and it is said that a retainer of King Tang 湯王, whose name was Yi Yin 伊尹, crept into the palace of King Jie of the Xia Dynasty* and

---

* The original script incorrectly states "King Zhou of the Zhou Dynasty."

overthrew him. It is also said that Sun Tzu 孫武, who wrote the famous book, *Art of War*, who was also a retainer of King Helü 闔閭 of the state of Wu 呉, used the five types of spy to defeat his enemies.

Gokan 五間: The Five Types of Spy

Inko no kan 因口之間： **Local Spies**
Their purpose is to gather information and to achieve their goals by using the local dialects. It is the same as the Japanese skill of *dakko* 奪口, which means, literally "ripping off the mouth" and is the method of spying, deceiving, or gathering information by having a good command of the local dialect.

Nairyo no kan 内良之間： **Inward Spies**
This refers to the method of secretly tempting an enemy retainer or someone who is close to the enemy and using them for one's own benefit. A good inward spy will carry out their mission in a thorough and precise way. However, the enemy may also use this technique on us, gaining one of our men as their ally. Furthermore, you can plant a spy within the enemy's ranks. This technique is also used in Japan as well as China. However, to do this, you need to prepare them years beforehand and with utmost care, managing and controlling them before they are actually needed.

Hantoku no kan 反徳之間： **Converted Spies**
This refers to getting ahold of the enemy's shinobi and using them for your own purposes. With their cooperation you can obtain remarkably outstanding information. In Japan it is called *kaerinin* or *sorinin* 反り忍. You can use the enemy's shinobi who have been sent to spy on you, by feeding them false information, thus, allowing them to falsely report back to your enemy.
Oral tradition says that:

If someone from the lower class speaks with more reason or intelligence than befits their status, you should be aware he might have been told to do so. You should observe people according to their type and discover if their words are true or false.

Shicho no kan 死長之間: "Doomed Spies" or "Those Who are Expendable"

It is said you should reward them liberally and they will work to bring about critical benefits for your army's need.

Tensei no kan 天生之間: Surviving Spies

This refers to spies who are good at espionage and spying by infiltrating enemy lines.

The above are the so-called *gokan*, five types of spy and these are called shinobi in Japan. Their philosophy is universal to both countries, even though they have been labeled differently in China.

This is the end of the five types of spy and their origin in China.

Kyodo 郷導 (how to be guided by locals)

This refers to situations when you don't know the enemy's district. It is the art of building a rapport with local inhabitants, be aware that even an idiot living in that region would be more helpful than an outsider who insists he knows the place very well. You should ask a local inhabitant for information when you are in an unfamiliar area. It is said in ancient times that Sasaki Saburo Moritsuna 佐々木三郎盛綱, during the Genpei War, was in the area of Kojima of the Bizen province and was preparing to attack more than 500 people of the Heiji area who were stuck on an island. Moritsuna obtained vital coastal information from a local inhabitant on the seaside who told him how to safely cross the channel using shallower areas. He did this by giving the local inhabitant a *shirosayamaki* sword 白鞘巻 with silver fittings. After acquiring this information, he killed the man out of a need for secrecy. This is an example of using *kyodo*.

Togiki 外聞 (hearing information from the outside)

This is the method of not entering too deeply into the enemy's territory while still coming to a logical conclusion by gathering information from the outside. In fact, you can deduce the enemy's disposition by gathering various kinds of information thoroughly while still not crossing their boundaries. Considering all factors together, you can attain a rough picture of their motives in advance. However, you should be careful, ensure that the informers have not been planted to feed you misinformation.

Shinobi No Mono 忍者

This refers to Japanese spies; they never feel hesitant about their business, they spy whether it is daytime or at night. They are the same as *nusubito* in skill, however a ninja does not steal [for profit.] Those who have mastered the shinobi arts can creep into any difficult situation and return, even if there is no way back. It should be said that their mastery is extremely profound.

Nusubito 盗人

They have a natural audacity, have no reasoning ability and lack the power of judgment about future events. They are similar to a hunter who is too absorbed in pursuing a deer and fails to see the mountains around him. They are not aware of the possibility of ruining themselves through stealing. Alas, how artless and thoughtless they are! We shall not talk of their art.

Understanding What is Required to Follow the True Path of the Shinobi

正忍記一流之次第

Shoninki Ichiryu no Shidai

The mystery of the ninja and their arts appears not only to be a fantasy today but also during the heyday of the shinobi themselves. After describing what types of shinobi exist in the world, Natori feels that he must tell the reader about what the ninja can and cannot do. He does this in a magnificent way via a beautiful dialogue between an ancient master and a hapless student. By using this short conversation, Natori gives us a taste of this deep and rich world, full of accursed moonshine, hideous mountain hags, and bloodstained shinobi running through the wild woods. Through this vivid visual he demonstrates the folly of thinking that a ninja is superhuman and instructs his pupil that a ninja is only a man, though he is a man with the pure strength given to him by solitude, perseverance, and determination—qualities we could all use and qualities he wishes to teach us.

The Master Says:

Try hard, try hard! The true mastery of the shinobi arts is difficult to attain. The masters of the past prepared themselves when leaving home for the eventuality that they might not see their beloved wife and children again. If they did manage to get home then they appreciated that they had barely escaped death thanks to the intervention of fate, hence, the reason for the ideogram for the shinobi, which is constructed of the symbol of a heart under a blade.

Alas, how sad it is! Even if you have mastered millions of skills and know them like the back of your hand, this path of the shinobi will leave you uncertain, you will be wanting to attain even more knowledge than you have. If you approach it too casually, you will be making a serious mistake, as nothing is more horrifying than this path.

The Apprentice Replies:

I have vaguely heard that the arts of the shinobi will enable you to creep into forbidden places or jump over a barrier that is meant to prevent you from escaping. Even if a father, a son, or brothers see each other, they would not be able to recognize each other while they are engaged in ninja covert acts. I have also heard that even if shinobi are seen from the front, even then, in the next moment they might attack you from behind, or while you assume they are behind you, you could lose sight of them again from moment to moment.

Don't all these factors owe their marvel to the artistry of the mysterious path and the subtleties of this marvelous art of ninjutsu? What tradition could make it possible to realize such wonders like these? Surely this art cannot be attained by mere human beings? Please Master, teach me the truth of ninjutsu.

The Master Answers:

What kind of art, or what kind of reason have you heard in order to so misunderstand this path? Nothing is mystical about the true tradition and correct way of ninjutsu. Sometimes, the mind is substantial (*jitsu*) 実 and form and reality are insubstantial (*kyo*) 虚, this is the idea of truth and emptiness. At other times it is reversed, form is substantial while the mind is insubstantial. Every master of the shinobi arts has a "silver tongue" and is always eloquent according to needs of the situation.

The ninja can do the following things: sometimes talk about a province they have never been to, tell a strange story about a place they don't know, pretend to be friends with a stranger, buy things with gold or silver they don't have, eat food nobody gives, get drunk and go on a drunken spree without drinking alcohol, and learn every kind of art in the world. Also, oddly without being asked, they disguise themselves as a monk or *Yamabushi* mountain priest, even if they are not used to doing it; they have nowhere they cannot go; they camouflage themselves as women, such as an old mountain hag; they go out acting covertly all night and sleep out in the wilderness without shelter. Also, sometimes as a ninja, you may be startled at the call of a deer and search in panic for a hiding place while moaning in agonizing pain or grief or a sadness of which no one is aware. You will get annoyed with the moonlight and seek for the shelter of the shadows within a forest. Yet you have nobody to talk with or to unburden such toils and dismay, are any of these things a marvel for you at all? The people of the world around you may not know of your plight and engage you in conversation, but you must answer them, making comments on the truth of matters, this is also one of the deceptions of the shinobi.

The "insubstantial" (*fujitsu* 不実) also includes the "substantial" (*jitsu* 実) within itself, this is a key to the realization of the true way of the shinobi, so do not get lost on the wrong path or be blinded or discredited by false ideas, help yourself to understand that you must keep within the true principles of this tradition.

PART TWO

The Shoninki Opening Chapters

正忍記初巻

Shoninki Sho Kan

The opening chapters deal with what we would classify as the archetypal ninja methods, here Natori outlines the basic tools and weapons of the ninja, then he goes on to concentrate on infiltration in its many forms, from the iconic arts of stealthy night missions to placing yourself in the line of fire by entering the world of the undercover agent and infiltration unit. Showing you how to work in teams or as a solo-shinobi, The opening chapters set the standard needed to become a true and master ninja.

The Equipment and Outfits for Shinobi Activities

忍出立の習

Shinobu Idetachi no Narai

Natori has described what the shinobi are and what they can and cannot do. Now we enter the world of what a shinobi needs: his tools, his methods of disguise and the different methods of ninjutsu that he must learn. First, a field agent must have his six basic tools, the weapons of the ninja's "espionage artillery." With these in hand, the ninja must master the seven basic disguises that will allow him to move around the restrictive Japanese country with ease, allowing him to gain entry into places where he should not be and to talk to people he should not be talking to. Having the tools of the trade and the outward manifestation of other people, the shinobi soldier must now understand the weaknesses that people possess, weaknesses found through a shared liking for the five basic loves in life. Having built the ninja up to this level, Natori now sees that they are instructed on the ten ancient ways of the shinobi principles, giving them the ammunition that they need to deceive people and render them pliable to the will of the ninja.

The underlying principle of the shinobi is to not be discovered by others. Therefore, you should provide yourself with those outfits that will change the way you look. Masters of the shinobi arts in ancient times were scarcely recognizable, even between a father and son or between brothers, even more so if they were unrelated to the ninja.

Basically, there are six items of essential gear for shinobi:

1. The deep and wide straw hat called the *amigasa* あミ笠
2. The grappling hook known as a *kaginawa* かぎ縄
3. A stone pencil we call a *sekihitsu* 石筆
4. Field medicine called *kusuri* 茉り
5. A three-foot (90 cm) piece of cloth called a *sanjaku tenugui* 三尺手拭
6. A fire-starting implement called an *uchitake* 打竹 or *tsuke-take* 附竹

The *amigasa* straw hat is used to cover your face or change your appearance, while still allowing you to see other people.

The *kaginawa* grappling iron is used to climb up or descend from a height; to grapple or restrain and tie someone up, to lock a sliding door and for many other purposes not mentioned here. There is a thin rope called a *konawa* and this school has a secret technique that we use and it can also secure the saddle of a horse if needed. The methods for using this rope should be passed down in accordance with the needs for any specific situation.

The *sekihitsu* stone pencil is used to take notes or make marks.

The medicine is called worm's killer* and is an essential tool. If you get sick in the field, you will not be able to accomplish your task, so you should carry it with you at all times.

The *sanjaku tenugui* cloth is very useful as a *hachimaki* head-band, you can wrap it around your head and around your face, and you may use it to extend a sash by tying them together to make a rope so that you may climb a wall or other heights. In other

---

* At that time, people thought stomach aches or food poisoning were caused by worms.

schools you are supposed to always keep it inside your *obi* sash. In my school however, you should fold it up and keep it inside your collar, even when you wear the lightweight summer *katabira* 帷子 kimono, it is essential that you should always keep one of these cloths about you at all times.

The *tsuketake* 附竹 fire starter is a tool that helps you to create fire; this can be used when you need to have a fire at night. Among the different types of fire-starting equipment the *donohi* 胴火 body-warming device is a most favorable asset. Also, it can be used for the skill of *jiyaki* 地焼, scorched earth policy. Also, you can use it for arson and other purposes.

The color of your clothes should be one of the following colors: brown, tan (this is called *numerigaki*), black, or navy blue. These are so common that it is hard to stand out while wearing them. You can use the *amabaori*, raincoat, or a cape to change your appearance and body shape. Whenever you steal up on someone you had better carry an *o-wakizashi* 大脇差 short-sword. Sometimes you need to cover your sword blade in ink.* Your *obi* sash should be black, with two garments sewn together with slip stitches, this is called *waobi*. This is done because it is advised that you should quickly take hold of the end without fumbling.

Shichihode 七方出
The Seven Types of Disguise a Ninja Should Use

1. *Komuso* Zen monks こむ僧: you will be able to wear the straw *amigasa* hat in this get up, which as mentioned before, it will give you good visibility while hiding your face.
2. *Shukke* monks 出家: this is an easy approach for both men and women to use.
3. *Yamabushi* mountain priests 山伏: this is an easy approach for both men or women to use and they can carry a *katana* or *wakizashi* short-sword without being questioned.

---

* *Mi* 身 can be read as "sword blade" or "body." It is unknown which meaning Natori wished to employ and can be taken as "to ink the body," i.e., exposed skin, or "to ink the sword blade."

4. A merchant: This makes it easy to approach people.
5. *Hokashi* street entertainers ほうか師: This will make it easy to approach people as they commonly do street entertainment and people are used to them traveling.
6. *Sarugaku* performers さるがく: As a form of theater, people will not question why you are there.
7. *Tune no katachi* or street clothes つねノ形: You should dress in accordance to the type of person you wish to emulate and that will be found on the streets that you wish to travel along.

The above are the types of appearances you can successfully imitate. You should choose the identities that would best suit your personality and demeanor so that you can remain unperturbed throughout your shinobi mission.

According to Kiichi, who practiced esoteric cosmology and founded a sword school, there are five kinds of things that people like:

1. Beautiful men and women
2. Luxury palaces and mansions
3. Beautiful and quiet scenery consisting of rocks and water
4. *Dengaku* 田楽, which is a type of field music and folk dance
5. The fine arts, literature and calligraphy

If you come up with a plan that includes one of the above five, you will not fail to take in your enemy. It is said there would be no way for you to fail if you use these five elements.

The Following are Ten Ancient Ways of the Shinobi

1. *Onsei-nin* 音聲忍 ninjutsu by voice: A quietness of voice should be used in this style which includes *baiboku* バイ木 mouth gags and *dakko* 奪口, which is the skill of using a local dialect, alongside these two there is also eaves-

dropping and music.

2. *Jun-nin* 順忍 obedient ninjutsu: Gathering information by following people extensively, but not in a manner that will alert them or put them on their guard.

3. *Mushoho-nin* 無生法忍 zero attachment ninjutsu: This is done by causing disorder and taking advantage of the new situation and then acquiring an advantage from the opportunities you have made.

4. *Jogen-nin* 如幻忍 illusion-like ninjutsu: Taking advantage of even the smallest gap in the opponent's defense, it is essential to be fast with this method.

5. *Joei-nin* 如影忍 shadow-like ninjutsu: To get close to and stay near people and objects by hiding in the shadows.

6. *Joen-nin* 如焰忍 flare-like ninjutsu: Getting into people's minds when they let their guard down, and utilizing their weakness, this is also the case with houses and gaining entrance to them.

7. *Jomu-nin* 如夢忍 dream-like ninjutsu: You can deceive people at night with this style.

8. *Jokyo-nin* 如響忍 echo-like ninjutsu: To investigate the opponent's location employing local aspects to your own benefit.

9. *Joge-nin* 如化忍 disguise or mutation ninjutsu: Deceiving people. You can read their thoughts by pretending to be a run-of-the-mill person, putting them off their guard by disguising your appearance and gaining information via their trust.

10. *Joku-nin* 如空忍 void or empty-like ninjutsu: Deceiving people without them knowing or getting a hint at what you are up to and not allowing them to realize what has happened and how they have been used.

The above principles hold true through all the chapters that make up the *Shoninki*. You should use everything you have learned from them and apply them to all the lessons in this book. Therefore, I have written these in the first chapter even though they are of vital importance no matter where you are in the book. A depth of mind should be kept and reason should be held elevated above all things. As a ninja you should always have an awareness of the environment around you.

Walking Along Unfamiliar Mountain Paths

しらぬ山路の習

Shiranu Yamaji no Narai

Walking along the familiar streets of our modern world, we forget what life would be like in an unmapped medieval landscape. Through snowstorms and dead ends, the author gives us methods for operating in this medieval madness. Filled with fundamental facts and observations, we find out how to: travel on mountain paths and abandoned highways; circumvent dead ends; trust in fate when in the dark and you are lost in the wilderness; trust in the gods; learn from nature; and have faith in your mastery of the arts to get you through the dark times ahead.

There are no words to describe the feeling of uncertainty that comes from walking along an unfamiliar mountain path or in a dark forest. Neither is there anyone you can ask for information without giving yourself away. What can you do if you can find no clue anywhere around you that points to the route you should take? How can you choose a way through the unknown before you? To cope with this situation you should ask yourself the above question with a sensitive mind.

There are traditional ways to do this: If you come to a crossroads in the mountains and do not know which way to take, instead of dwelling on it you should recite an old verse, the first one that flashes into your mind. Then count how many syllables in the verse and choose to go right if it's odd and go left if it's even and do not have any doubts about the decision in the end.

This is because if you simply use the first thing that flashes through your head without any intention or contemplation, you are consigning yourself to divine intervention and fate. Wonders can happen when you abandon your ego.

It is said that along main roads you are likely to find castoff *waranji* straw sandals or shoes for horses or even shoes for cows that have been abandoned. You can also see dung quite often. Those roads where many people travel always have the ground padded down, and those that have but only a few people that ever travel along them have the soil exposed and soft. In fact, even if it is a main broad street with ample room there is always a thin pathway beaten into it by the people who use it.

There is a way to recognize a well-traveled path by observing the grasses and trees around the area. That is, you should look for mowed grass or stubbed or cut trees. Specifically, by seeing how recent or how old the damage is, you could know if a village is nearby or not. If people cut grass on a regular basis or if you notice that the fields are terraced then this means a village is located nearby. If birds and animals are easily startled, this is another sign that the road is well trodden. A smart person would never miss any of these things.

These are some things you can do if you have to walk along a snowy path. If you can see someone walking ahead of you, you should keep watching his or her back. If a horse is walking along the same path, you should keep watching its back as well. Do not look at the sky or look around continuously, as this may lead you to make mistakes. Sometimes you cannot help but be caught in a snowstorm. If the heavy snow buries the path, it will be hard for you to see the tracks of other people along the way. To know the depth of the accumulated snow, you should stick a cane into snow beneath you. Even if the path is covered in snow, if the bottom is hard, you can assume that the path is heavily used. If a mountain path is hidden from you beneath the snow, you should stick to the lower half of the mountain. Be careful, if you walk where you only suspect there to be a path, you should be aware that you could fall into a valley at any time. If you have to walk along an unfamiliar road covered with snow, there is a traditional way to follow the path. You should have a horse walk in front of you; the reason for this is as follows:

A retainer of Duke Huan of Qi, from Guan Zhong in China went to fight against the ancient Chinese state of Gu-zhu while they had a period of heavy snow. He said that an old horse would know the path and so he had one go ahead of them and they could follow it as it made its way home, becoming a guide for the troops.

There is a tradition of knotting grasses to make markings that map where you have been; you should utilize anything that will help you make a mental note, you should make marks using markers, noting landmarks, or leaving footsteps, etc. If you come to a dead end, you should go back to where it begins and take another path at once without delay.

It is cold when it snows, thus, you should use a *donohi* body warmer. This is not only for protection from the cold, but you can always use it for other purposes depending on your needs. To make one, take a copper cylinder of 5 or 6 *sun* (6 to 7 inches) in length and 4 or 5 *sun* (5 to 6 inches) in circumference, then put closing caps on both ends. Put any form of openwork on the end of these caps, and then, form slots on the cylinder to let air in and warmth seep out.

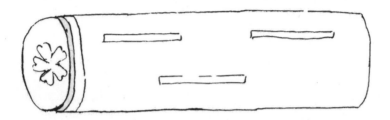

Firmly twist hemp of cotton—which has been well rinsed in water and kneaded by hand—around a thin iron rod, then remove the rod, make sure that the width of the rolled cloth fits into the cylinder and then place it into a closed pot, roast until it goes black. Finally wrap it all in paper. Cut it the same length as the cylinder and you are ready to now ignite the end. *Sugiharagami* is a thin type of paper made of mulberry, this type of paper will also do as a wick. When twisting it, you can sometimes add a flammable component to sustain the fire for a prolonged period of time. The final recipe is up to your ingenuity. Therefore, the more often you make it, the longer you will be able to keep the device ignited and the more experienced you will become.

Other materials you can use are old tanned paper, eggplant stems and leaves, the bark of trees, bistort, seed of persimmons, decaying boards, and so on and so forth. Roll the previous ingredients around the iron core inside hemp of cotton material and then roast them until they are black. In case you only need it as a body warmer, bistort would be fine. It will stay alight for 6 or 7 *toki*, which can be around 12 to 14 hours.

Walking at Night

夜道の事

Yomichi no Koto

Like the samurai and his sword, the ninja and the darkness of night go hand-in-hand. What must a ninja do when he sees torchlight on the horizon? Or crouched figures in the darkness? Our modern perception of the ninja is that he is the master of stealth and can maneuver easily in the shroud of night. Academics and ninja enthusiasts around the world have debated the validity of this trait, but these debates end here. Natori tells us that the shinobi was a man who operated most efficiently in the dead of night; he hid in the shadows of a moonless forest, clashed with swords in the pitch dark, and tasted the earth to find his way in the inky night. He teaches the ninja how to listen for the ten distinct steps of the people of the world, identifying who was coming along the road before they could be seen. Also, how to replicate those steps so the ninja could deceive others who wanted to track him down.

Though it is easier to work more stealthily at night than in the daytime, the drawback is that people could easily consider you as acting in a "fishy" manner or they will be suspicious if they catch you skulking around at night. Therefore, you should be very careful when involved in covert nighttime activities.

If you can hardly see what lies ahead of you while walking along a street at night, you should sit down on the ground and duck down to see the skyline from a lower point. This will allow you to look from an angle up towards the clouds and the sky, which will give you a better picture.

Well-traveled roads taste salty, remember this if you taste them.

If there are lots of fence posts ahead of you, you could mistake them for human beings. To avoid this you have to try to watch very carefully. If they are human, they will not all be the same height unlike fence posts, which are uniform in height. You could also mistake grass or trees for people when it's dark. If they are human, they will move after a while. However, if you do not concentrate well enough or do not have a still mind, you will mistake grasses and trees as people everywhere you turn. To prevent this you should just stay still, watching for a while, waiting in the dark. If you keep watching long enough, people will always move in the end, as they can only remain motionless for a short time, this is how you tell if there is an opponent in the dark.

When you see the firelight of a lantern, duck down, hold your sword upright on the ground and put a folded fan on the end of the sword horizontally like a "T" shape, so that you can see the fire just on the top line of the fan. If the light is going away from you, it will ascend above the fan, if it is coming towards you it goes down. You can also know if it is going right or left.

When you walk with a servant holding a light, you should walk directly in front of him and in his shadow to protect your night vision. When someone is approaching, keep the light toward the direction that he or she is coming from so that you can stay in the darkness. At the time of a sword battle, be sure to have the light from the torch over the enemy as much as possible or to keep the light as close to the enemy as you can. This makes it easy for you to sneak around to the back of the enemy while their night vision is disrupted.

When you light a fire in a dark house, you shouldn't be careless and make it too abruptly, as it will blindingly glare around you killing your night vision to the point where you can hardly see what lies just a few feet away from you. Therefore, you should gradually bring it out from the shadow of your body and then let the light shine outwards while your night vision gets used to the light.

When you walk at night, if the moon is bright, you should pass in the shadows where you can. If you come across someone and don't want to be seen, you should keep in the shadows and put your hand across your face, so that they cannot see your face in the moonlight.

Most people say that you shouldn't wear *setta* sandals at night and that it's a foolish thing to do. It has to be advised however, that it isn't always a careless thing to wear *setta* at night at all; in fact, sometimes it is a positive thing. You can tell who is walking around by the sound of their footsteps. One of the shinobi skills is to sometimes vary their footsteps in the dark; this technique is called *kutsukae* 沓替え, which means, "changing your footwear."

There are ten variations of this type of deceptive stepping:

1. *Nukiashi* ぬき足   — Stealthy footsteps where you pull up your feet
2. *Suriashi* すり足   — Sliding your feet along the ground
3. *Shimeashi* しめ足   — The tip-toe gait, this is where you restrain your footsteps or tighten your walk
4. *Tobiashi* 飛足   — A form of bounding
5. *Kataashioto* 片足音   — A limping walk
6. *Oashi* 大足   — Walking with long strides

7. *Koashi* 小足   — Walking with short strides
8. *Kizamiashi* きざみ足   — Chopping steps
9. *Hashiriashi* はしり足 — Running
10. *Tsunenoashi* 常の足   — Normal walking

Infiltrating a Forbidden Mansion

禁宿取入ル習

Kinshuku Toriiru Narai

One of the iconic images of the ninja is that of a creeping figure gaining entrance into a forbidden place, climbing a wall and entering the home of the target. Later, Natori deals with this traditional image, but here, in this next chapter, he shows that a ninja would need an even sterner backbone than we first thought. Here he describes deception in the most casual but dangerous way possible: To walk up and simply enter a house under false pretenses or to join an army on the march or even to ask the intended target for aid and shelter, when, in fact, you are plotting against him.

One legendary feat of the ninja has always been their amazing ability to count and survey enemy troops and give accurate descriptions of their strength of arms. The secrets are simple but effective and also show how a shinobi could walk amongst the opposition counting and taking statistics without ever thinking of a single number. Remembering that capture or discovery would result in torture, if not execution, the spirit of a shinobi soldier must have been solid to the core. Calmly infiltrating and conversing with the enemy without a fear of death displays a level of courage rarely replicated in today's world.

Even if you have been to a place before, you may still feel uneasy if the area is quite unfamiliar. This is even more so with a forbidden or restricted area. It is essential for the shinobi to know how to get into such mansions without difficulty or fear; it is one of the essential things a ninja must know.

In another province, sometimes you have to make an educated guess about the building complex that you need to infiltrate. Such buildings maybe strictly forbidden to outsiders. It is best for you to walk by the gate a few times with a phony intention in mind. One method of getting information is to feign illness in front of the gate, take a rest there and have your servant or accomplice ask the inhabitants for medicine, hot water, or simply just cool water. Choose a sudden illness such as *omushi* 大虫 (stomach ache), *kakuran* 霍乱 (sudden vomiting), *gansho* 含傷 (food poisoning), epilepsy, or diarrhea or something else along these lines. Though, being drunk would not be proper at all and you should never pretend to be so in this situation. After you have been given what you asked for and have feigned recovery, you should go in to your target area to say thank you so that you become acquainted with them, and leave without pushing your luck.

At a later date, you may come back, giving the occupants presents to show your gratitude for their help; flatter and get intimate with them. Basically, when you visit someone's place you should praise their children as an effective way to gain entry. When you give presents, don't forget to give one to the master's wife first. Next you should treat his favorite servant(s), whether they are men or women. The master will be pleased about that, rather than having one gift just for him, he sees that his people are happy and this will influence him. Thus, in this way you could glean information about what you want while talking to the people of the mansion.

An oral tradition says that you should test metal with fire and humans with words.

The uguisu (Japanese bush warbler) that chirps among blossoms
is fragrant like blossoms even though they are not even flowers.

The poem above means that if you creep into someone's favor with smooth words, you can deduce valuable information even from the smallest of small talk.

To estimate the area of a place, you should figure it out by multiplying any distance you do know for sure or that at which you can take an educated guess. To know the number of houses within a compound, you should prepare two bags of a certain number of pebbles or beans and write that amount on each bag. Now, with one bag up each sleeve you have walk around and discard a pebble or bean for each house individually. If it's an unoccupied house, you take one from the left sleeve and if it's a house with inhabitants, from the right sleeve, be careful and do not mix them up. Then, when you have finished, count the number left in the bags and subtract it from the original number that you had at the start. This way you can know the exact number of houses within the compound without having to count them. You can also apply this technique to counting the numbers of people in a procession. In this case, you will have to use a higher number of bags for such things as: foot soldiers, mounted warriors, spearmen, etc. Make sure to put more pebbles than the numbers you expect so that you do not run out half way through. When you do the counting, you should position yourself at a place where they have to walk in single file so that you have a good view and enough time to count them, places such as narrow tracks or a bridge would be good for this.

If it is difficult for you to get the whole picture, slip among the retinue or pretend to be a merchant accompanying the army and act as if you wish to accompany them for a couple of days of trade. How could you ever fail to count them within this period? A few days is more than you need. Be careful to take every measure possible. When infiltrating an army you should engage with no one but the servants. Treat them liberally and do favors for them without allowing them to know you are being deceitful.

Nothing could be worse than your intentions becoming too easily detected. Be warned, even if you could gain the favor of a higher-ranking person, it would prevent you from achieving the desired effect that you originally wanted. This is because you will be hated by the lower-ranking people for the favor you are being shown by those above you.

Learning from Foxes and Wolves

狐狼ノ道ノ習

Korō no Michi no Narai

Today, in our capitalist world, where time is money and money is time, we instinctively search for the quickest route, the easy way out, and the trajectory that gets the best results. The ninja were taught the exact opposite: patience, perseverance, and careful planning is more important than the useless observation of the passing of time. Here we see that if a ninja needed to cross a barrier they would walk for miles to find an alternative route, in comparison to the quick and "easy" path. By studying the alertness and guile of animals such as the fox, a shinobi would be quick-witted and cunning, he would learn the routes, tracks and ways of the people of all the provinces around him, studying other cultures and integrating with those who are different. This way the ninja would move through an ever-changing world, a shadow in time, adapting to the world around him.

Foxes and wolves are of the smartest of animals. It is said that foxes will often fool people and that wolves read people's minds. This is because they can walk the most difficult of paths, invent unimaginable ideas, and do numerous marvelous tasks; you should learn from their ways.

When you come across a checkpoint in the enemy's province, one that inspects both outgoing and incoming traffic, do not try to pass through it by different methods or skills. You should do as foxes and wolves do and try to find a bypass. Even by going 2 or 3 *Ri*, which is 5–7.5 miles (8–12 km) away from the checkpoint, you will always find a side road frequented by the locals. If necessary you should choose to disguise yourself as a *shukke, yamabushi*, merchant or anything else that you feel is appropriate to the situation. Pilgrims have a good reason to move around shrines and temples. For this purpose, which is different from other cases, it may be better for you to move as a company of two or three people. In such cases, the technique of *dakko* 奪口, to understand all the local customs and dialects, is used.

Originally, the skill of *dakko* was to imitate the dialects of more than 60 provinces with a great fluency. Those skilled knew and were aware of all the points of interest, historic spots and famous places of natural beauty within each area. Thus, it is called *dakko*, "depriving the world with your mouth." However, this technique used to be achieved only by ancient masters and seems to be too difficult for people of the present time to master completely. Your efforts could be easily interpreted as *hatonokai* 鳩のかひ, the tricks of street con men, and thus could be self-damaging after all your effort. Therefore, you should be very careful in using this.

Learning from Cattle
and Horses

牛馬ノつたへの事

Gyūba no Tsutae no Koto

*In direct contrast to the last chapter, Natori gives us an alternative to
the guile and splendor of the fox and calls on an unusual animal from
which to gain inspiration: the beast of burden. Although hidden beneath the text, this method is one of the ninja's most underhanded and
unchivalrous methods of operation, perhaps adding to their reputation
as honorless thieves and brigands. To be like a horse or a cow and to
be led straight to the enemy headquarters as an emissary or messenger
must have taken courage that is difficult to comprehend and that we
find hard to display in our own lives. Besides being a demonstration
of iron nerves, it shows us that sometimes we can ride on the coattails
of others and travel in the wake of their effort.*

In this technique, you'll be using the way of cattle and horses, as opposed to that of foxes and wolves. Here you behave as though being tamed and show yourself openly in front of people's eyes.

To do this, the commander of your side should send a shinobi no mono to the enemy general as a messenger or a servant accompanying an envoy. This is called the "way of cattle and horses," as they are led and guided by the people of the enemy camp, allowing you to freely walk along the roads on the way to investigate the enemy.

The shinobi no mono, who is accompanying the messenger, should wander around various places or stay in certain areas of that province according to the situation at hand. This is where you need to use your wits and resources to the fullest. For example, you could make up an excuse, such as that you have a relative in the area, and then pretend to visit them, or to feign an illness, or act as if you are going to betray and defect from your own province, blaming your master and praising the enemy province, and so on and so forth. All is dependent on your wit and should be in accordance to the situation at all times.

Gathering Information at Shrines and Temples

宮寺計聞ノ習

Kyuji Keibun no Narai

The main job of the ninja is not that of an assassin, as some may think. In fact, it is postulated that the ninjas of Natori's school of ninjutsu were experts in all forms of espionage and infiltration. In a secular world and lifestyle, we may find it hard to comprehend the reality of a temple or a place of worship as a major hub for gossip and information networks. However, in a world where religion is fundamental to daily life, the priests and monks, as men of the cloth, hold key positions— they make it their business to understand what is happening within their own community. If money and religion go hand-in-hand, so does knowledge and power, and if knowledge is power, then a shinobi must tap into that at its source. That source was, for the feudal shinobi, the shrines and temples of the Japanese highways.

There are no better places than shrines and temples for trying to investigate what is happening within a said province and to acquire the information you want. For this purpose you should give the priests or other men of the cloth gold and silver coins generously, sparing no expense. If you give ordinary people gold and silver, they will become suspicious of you because this is not normal. However, Buddhist or Shinto priests, if given silver and gold, will not suspect you at all but instead will be delighted to accept it and offer to treat you with meals and hospitality. Taking advantage of this opportunity, you should probe them for information while getting them drunk.

If you "get wind" of a rebellious plot, you should ask your hosts if they have any plans to construct a new building to pray for the fulfilment of someone's wishes, suggesting and hinting at your willingness to help financially. Let them talk on about their hopes, enough to loosen their tongues. Then they will not be able to stop themselves from bragging about their wonderful religious power or the divine wonders, and then they will give away everything you need to know at great length. During their attempts to make you donate for their cause, they are likely to make a display of their knowledge as a show of power. Thus, by exploiting their very nature, you can attain your goal.

To know what the people in any given province are thinking and what the situation is within the area, you should go and eavesdrop at an *ageya* 揚屋, this is a licensed house of assignation where the highest rank of courtesans are appointed to their clients, or at the public baths, or a *keiseiya* 傾城屋 brothel or a gambling den and so on. There are no secrets that cannot be revealed at places such as these.

Changing Your Appearance

変化之論

Henge no Ron

Transmutation and disappearance are the traits given to the mythical ninja by the media and the superstitious peasant. However, these traits are easy enough to see in our modern reality. After all, countless actors play countless roles in an endless procession of plays and films. A good actor can take you into an alternate reality for the duration of the performance—the illusion of acting can create a world beyond our own. This skill, one we are so accustomed to in our modern world, when applied in a world with no media communications, no photography, and no way to know the face of another without seeing it first hand, would give a masterful actor a gullible and naive audience. It is here that the ninja assumes the guise of any alter ego that he so desires and it is here that a chosen pseudonym can gain entrance into places that other skills cannot.

According to tradition and legend, foxes and raccoon dogs can transform themselves to trick people. How could people acquire the same skill you may wonder? There should be no way that you can transform your appearance or mutate into a different form. This would be a vast mistake and is proof that you are overconfident of your own intellect and perceive other people as lower in intelligence than yourself. If you assume you have mastered such a dubious way and believe it to be true and then pass it on to others, you will fail at a critical point. Therefore, you should be fully aware of the risk while attempting to gain learning in this technique.

To change your appearance during your covert activity, it is useful to wear a long *haori* jacket or a rain cape. If you can reshape your eyebrows, blacken your teeth with dies, change the shape of your hairline on the forehead, wear Japanese black ink on your face, tousle your hair, and put some tresses in your mouth, then your face will look different. There are some pigments you can apply to your face.

Below are three recipes for making colors.

1. Take *usuzumi* うす墨 (gray ink), with *shu* 朱 (vermilion red), which is made from cinnabar and lastly, mix in standard *oshiroi* おしろい (white face make-up powder).
2. Take *usu'oshiroi* (diluted white face make-up) with *kiwada* きわだ or 黄檗 (yellow). This is made from the bark of the amur cork tree which belongs to the citrus family, its bark is used as medicine or pigmentation. Then add *shu* 朱 (vermilion red), and *odo* 黄土 (yellow ochre).
3. Take *usukiwada* (pale yellow) with *beni* 紅 (red) and *airo* 藍蝋 (indigo). This last one is a dark blue dye obtained from fermented leaves of the indigo plant.

Blend the colors as mentioned above and try some on your skin. Application should be avoided if it doesn't naturally fit into the theme of your face. A false beard should often be used as it hides your features.

You should be aware that if you pretend to be crippled but can't perform the imitation very well, your attempts will easily be identified. You sometimes need to fake an illness at short notice; here are some ways to help your performance: don't sleep at night to induce sleep deprivation, have moxa treatment burnt on to your skin, fast to the utmost limit that you can so that you look emaciated, leave your beard unshaven and hair uncut, don't clip your nails and toenails, don't clean your body, wear less clothing and wear a *hachimaki* headband with a thin piece of string. Pretending to be sick is called *kyobyo* 虚病. Besides these examples, there are numerous kinds of things you could do according to the situation at hand. You should keep learning this skill with the greatest care.

Hints for Infiltrating
an Enemy's Position

陣中忍時之習
Jinchū Shinobu Toki no Narai

When an enemy battle camp is spotted, then the master has to decide how he might best counter this strengthening of opposition. One way is to build up a strength of arms that surpasses those of his enemy, or by acquiring detailed information of the enemy's strengths and weaknesses so that a smaller force could effectively rout the army. The best way to get that vital information is in the use of spies. For feudal Japan, this job fell to the ninja. Undetected by the enemy, the ninja would wander through the enemy camp amassing troop numbers, battle plans, established routines, and any other information that could help his or her master dispel the opposition forces from the land. Natori breaks down this difficult task into two sections: advisable times and advantageous positions.

This skill set is of vital importance to the shinobi. Before you set off on a mission of infiltration, you should make arrangements with your allies for accommodations for your safe return journey, such as a preordained selection of smoke signals or light signals via a torch.

When you infiltrate the enemy's position you need to know what are the best times to "steal in." The optimum times to accomplish these tasks are as follows:

1. When lower-ranking soldiers are cutting down trees and bamboo, leaving them scattered around the area
2. While they are constructing their position, this will allow you to move around with ease
3. On a night when the enemy are exhausted after a day of fighting
4. During a rain storm

In any case, you should slip in among the lower-ranking soldiers. Do not slip in with the samurai 士 for they are formidable people who are fierce.

If you infiltrate at night, you should choose the hours of the Boar 亥 (9–11 pm) and the Rat 子 (11 pm–1 am) and also the last third of the hour of the Tiger 寅 (4:20 am–5 am). Or when horizontal clouds appear extending over the peaks of the mountains because this means dawn is approaching.

When you scout ahead and speak to someone within your area of infiltration, you should speak in the dialect of his or her province. Try to listen carefully to secure the enemy's password. Be warned, to counteract this technique in ancient times, people used to use:

1. *Tachisuguri Isuguri* 立すぐり居すぐり, this is the method of standing up or sitting down when a password is given to add extra security and to identify enemy spies who have infiltrated your group.

2. *Aijirushi* 相印, markings, emblems or signals; these are to identify the allies from the enemy.
3. *Aikotoba* 相言葉, the addition of supporting combination passwords.

In the situation where you are nearly detected, there is a useful way to escape final discovery, this is by using *toki no sodo, kake-goe no narai* 時のそうどう懸こゑの習, the skill of shouting and causing a distraction. This is done by creating a hassle and shouting loudly. To move around a group with haste, creating a quarrel, or making a vociferous fuss, saying, "Hey, it's a fight, it's a fight!" or any other distraction that makes sense at the time.

It is better for you to move from one place to another to help you to avoid being followed. However, you will be found out if you move thoughtlessly. If you are detected, you should leave it to fate and do not give in to fear.

Here is a selection of good hiding places: by an old well, behind a large stone, on a cliff, in the mountains, in a hollow or cave, in a toilet, behind a large tree, by sticking close to a wall, or alternately, by hiding in plain sight. You should also be aware that such places, which appear to be positive places to hide, are likely to draw suspicion from experienced people.

Learning from Waterfowl

水鳥之教

Mizudori no Oshie

Like a cat disturbing a bird from its serene seat on a branch, the ninja can disturb the natural wildlife around them, signaling to the enemy that danger is nearby. Natori dedicates this chapter as a warning to apprentice shinobi that even the smallest of creatures can give away your position and, in turn, that you too can identify an enemy in this fashion. Castle moats and the use of water in defensive systems can be seen in many cultures from around the world. Like animals, bodies of water are enemies to the ninja and need to be treated with care; a ripple out of place in the view of an alert guard could spell the end for a shinobi soldier.

Here are some hints about what are deemed as positive places for shinobi to hide, no matter which side of the war that they are on. Also, take into account the fact that no matter how busy your mind is beneath the surface, you must always appear graceful and calm to all, just as waterfowl do on a calm lake. There are those who uphold the true way of the shinobi, and they should stay on the path of perseverance, which makes them righteous, even though others around them disrespect the ways of the shinobi, thus can they not be described as saints or even as enlightened?

> *The waters in Jiang Nan are even bluer than that of heaven*
> *Where I found a gull, appearing to be as quiet as me*

> —From the Enga* collection of poetry
> by Shangu Daoren (1045–1105)

There are likely to be shinobi in places such as: lurking in the vicinity of a castle, or by the wall of a quay, or by a stone wall or in a rough spot. You should see if there are any waterfowl or animals to be found around that area. Be aware that they may take flight if they are startled by any noise you may make.

Like a wisp of smoke in the sky, if a *fushikamari* 伏陰り (one who lies down) scout is in hiding, birds will often avoid him, take flight and blanket the sky covering the starlight above just to shun him. A shinobi must always be careful about these things. It is for you to investigate a way to hide properly, using your own best judgment.

To cross the water with ease, make a square with four bamboo sticks, with each corner lashed together, and then fasten a calabash on each corner as buoyancy. Furthermore, in some cases, a tub can be used successfully as a flotation device to get across water in times of need.

When you hide within the water, allow only your face to surface and do this only within the shadows of the trees, while drawing reeds around you and your face. Furthermore, it is said,

---

* Presumably, this is the title of the collection of his poetry.

those who are good at diving carry a bamboo cylinder or the scabbard of a sword with a hole in the end, this is so that you can breathe through it from time to time while diving, taking breaths periodically as you come close to the surface. To cross over the moat surrounding a castle, you should utilize the corners and use them accordingly. When you climb up a stone wall, you should jab spikes into the masonry to create footholds and handholds, use such things as *Kogai* hairpins in sequence with a *Kaginawa* grappling iron, so that you can get hold of them both to aid your climb.

Appropriate Times to "Creep In"

忍入時分之時

Shinobiiru Jibun no Koto

One infamous skill for which the shinobi are universally famous is the ability to be able to tell if someone is feigning sleep or not. They are rumored to have the ability to listen at the thin wooden screens, and calculate how many people are asleep, and if any are waiting for you in false slumber. Having identified the occupants of the house and their status, a ninja is said to have the ability to creep on to the roof by using his sword as a foot hold and bringing it up after him by means of a cord, from here he is said to have wandered the rooftops of a compound, observing those below for his own ends. It is here that, for once, the media ventures into the realm of historical accuracy as Natori reveals the skills needed for such a "night out on the tiles."

There is no absolute correct time for the purpose of "creeping in," but you should aim for the time where the inhabitants of a house are most busy, that is the time when a person's guard is down. Be aware that "stealing in" should not be done at all in haste and never without enough care taken, lest you may fail.

The best times at night for this are around dusk, the hours of the Boar 亥 (9–11 pm), of the Rat 子 (11 pm–1 am), and of the Tiger 寅 (3–5 am).*

In the daytime, the optimum times are of the Hare 卯 (5–7 am), of the Horse 午 (11 am–1 pm), and of the Cock 酉 (5–7 pm).

If you don't know what time it is, it is possible for some people to tell the time by their body. When you breath more through your left nostril, then the time will be of an even number, and if the right then it will be an odd number.†

Even the iris of a cat's eyes are changeable according to the time of day, this is even more so with humans, thus the closer to midday you get then the narrower the eyes will be.

Most people go to bed no later than the time period of the Boar (9–11 pm) and get to sleep in the first third of the hour of the Ox (1 am–1:40 am) and wake in the first third of the Rabbit (5 am–5:40 am) though it is dependent on the individual person. If someone is truly asleep, his breathing will be irregular and you can discover if someone is feigning sleep if there is too much regularity to their breathing. It is also said people stir every two hours after they have fallen asleep.

Furthermore, tradition says that a house, as well as its occupants, also sleeps. That is, when the master of the house falls asleep so does the framework of the building and it appears to sink down. Therefore, there is a tradition handed down through the generations, this is where you dangle a small stone at the end of a thread and hang it at 5 or 6 *bu* (⅝–¾ inch, or 15–18 mm) above the ground in the morning. When the house "falls asleep" during the night, the stone will touch the floor.

---

* These times are dependent on the time of year and are to be considered approximations.

† Based on the Edo period time system.

How to get over a wall and pass through a hedge will be mentioned later, but to climb up onto the roof of a house, you should use a *kaginawa* grappling iron or you can use your *kantana* or *wakizashi* as a foothold.

In order to walk on a roof without making a sound, you should walk along the ridge* but not along the slope edges. If there is something strange in your way, you should throw a stone up on the roof first to see what it is, or simply just to make sure you are not seeing shadows and your eyes are not playing tricks on you.

The skill of avoiding capture when on a roof is called *ryo'ori* 両 おり this is a way you roll and drop a stone to one side of a house as you get down from the other side, this is done to add confusion and so that people will not know from which side you escaped.

---

* The text is ambitious here, it can be interpreted in two ways: firstly, to stay away from the edges and only use the ridge, or secondly, to cross over the ends and then move along the ridge. However, because of context we have chosen the former.

Lessons from the Four-Legged Animals

四足之習

Shisoku no Narai

If the dog is man's best friend, then they are the ninja's worst enemy! Natori gives here a whole chapter on the annoyance of dogs and animals as alarm systems to warn of infiltration agents. This chapter does support some age-old and semi-comical anecdotes such as: feeding guard dogs to befriend them, introducing a sexual distraction, or even going to the effort of poisoning the annoying animal to gain entrance to the place of infiltration. On a more serious note, it displays how aware and conscious of the details of the world around them the ninja had to be, to look at everything as a threat, problem, solution, or friend—a quality that shows how the ninja would live their art and master their skills as professionals.

This is about shinobi imitating dogs, a technique that is to be used on a dark moonless night only, so that you are never seen. You should be aware that humans have no way to copy the way that these animals physically look.

To impersonate dogs, you should be aware that they destroy walls or hedges by digging holes beneath them. Humans break through them directly. Dogs always growl to warn when they pass under a hedge. They also growl while sleeping or stretching themselves. They sometimes also tremble as they growl. To copy this, you pick up the hem of your kimono and shake it so that it will sound like dogs when they shake themselves. When dogs are facing down other animals, they are more likely to growl, while when threatening people, they tend to bark, make sure that you use the correct method.

When walking along a road, a dog will walk alongside the fence or a hedge. Be aware that in summer they like to lie in the shadows, and in winter, in the sun. For those dogs that threaten people and are great guard dogs, there is a technique called *ai'inu* 合犬. This is where you fix up a male dog with a female dog, or a female dog with a male dog, so that they will forget to threaten intruders and be more interested in mating. Or there is a commonly used technique of feeding them with grilled rice repeatedly beforehand, this is done to tame them and to befriend the animal. If you add some residue of the sesame seed, from which sesame oil has been extracted, it will deprive them of their voice and they will not be able to bark. It is said that if you feed them *machin* まちん, which is a poison derived from the seeds of the strychnine tree, they will become intoxicated and die through dehydration. However, if they drink water right afterwards they will revive themselves immediately. If iron filings are mixed in it, then they will die without fail. Those dogs that can endanger people a great deal are always annoying and disturbing for any shinobi during his stealth activities.

It is of less importance to impersonate cats than dogs. Some people can copy their calls but it is not as useful as copying dogs, so it is not necessary to explain this in detail here.

Two-Man Shinobi Teams

二人忍之事

Futari Shinobi no Koto

Natori's concerns here shine through more than his reliance on teamwork. More than ever, the martial artists of today shun teamwork, uniformity, and collaboration. They focus more on personal glory, making our concerns for the world the same as Natori's all those years ago. When two people cannot become one, then they will experience friction and discord. For a ninja, this friction or discord could be the difference between life and death. This being said, we see here that the skills and tricks the shinobi used while working in tandem and promoting teamwork can produce extraordinary results.

It is more difficult to do two-man teams than it is to do solo shinobi activities. To do this successfully, the two men should act with their minds together as one and make sure that there will be no misunderstandings in terms of the signs or measures between them. If there are any mistakes made by them, then it will take away any advantage that they may have had over solo shinobi missions.

As an example of acting in a two-man team, one shinobi knocks on the gate of the target house at night. When someone comes to answer, he takes flight in hope that the person of the house will chase him. In that moment, the other shinobi can creep through the gate.

Also, here is another example of a two-man technique, you should forge a letter or pretend to be a messenger from an acquaintance to lure the opponent out, so that you can get into the house. In this case, one acts as a messenger and the other creeps in. Or you could make a quarrel as a distraction. You can start a quarrel, and while one of you takes flight the other one runs into the target house to ask for shelter. Then, the other comes in after him and while he is talking to the occupants about the incident, the first one investigates what the inside of the house is like, or unlocks a door or a latchkey from within. As in this example, you should consider all possibilities and think the plan out thoroughly, depending on the situation you face.

Three-Man Shinobi Teams

三人忍之事

San'nin Shinobi no Koto

The modern concept of the ninja has changed since the ninja-boom of the late twentieth century, shifting from the role of master assassin to that of noble mountain warrior. This polar shift may have gone too far—Natori's instructions here bluntly demonstrate the ninja's outright skills as a street con artist and trickster. This acceptance of using trickery to deceive people and to take advantage of others can be seen in two lights: If the opposition is inherently bad or evil then the ninja's actions become courageous and hold merit; if the mission target is a group of innocents, then this displays evidence for a reputation as low-level scum, a reputation that the ninja possibly once held. Of course, this is totally dependent on the individual situation but it does give us an insight into the Eastern concept of In-Yo, *or Ying and Yang, as we commonly know it.*

The same holds true for this method as it does for two-man shinobi teams. Nothing is different; this is true with not only groups of three but also any number above that. It is necessary for all members of the team to be skilled. Since ancient times it has been known that as the number engaged in covert activity increases, then the covert activity will be more difficult to achieve.

It is vital to pull all the men's minds together to get good measured results. If any member of the group is dropping behind the other men, then the stronger ones will be impeded. Be aware that an unwise or under-skilled man can always do harm.

If three skilled people get together, would there be any difficulty when you steal into any place? If a wall or a fence stands in your way, two can stand side by side so that the other can mount it by standing on their shoulders. If he can succeed in scaling it, he can pull up the rest of the group from the top.

Or when one tries to steal into a place, the other two are there to aid the first person. One aid stands on watch while the other two carry out their mission. If you are near detection you should create a false thief, one person cries out "stop thief!" and then catches the supposed "thief," he apologizes for the "thief" to the occupants of the house and pretends to be a passerby. Or while trying to catch him, they can let him go deliberately, leaving the third man to explore.

This is similar to the case of the two-man shinobi team; it is even more effective to make a quarrel with three. Two shinobi should attract people's attention while the other slips into the target area. Or for example, you would have one ninja employed by the target and the other two install themselves in a temporary paid position within the household, such as to repair the inside of the house or so on, then there is nothing you could not do.

With three good men, there should be nothing that is impossible and you should contemplate thoroughly all possibilities available to you. Passwords or *aijirushi* 相印 identification marks should certainly be used, particularly when a high number of people are involved in the covert activity.

This is the end of the opening chapters.

PART THREE

The Shoninki Middle Chapters

正忍記中巻

Shoninki Chu Kan

Of the three main sections of the Shoninki, *the middle chapters are by far the most eclectic in content, instructing future shinobi on how to escape capture, how to use the environment and how to hide in the wilderness. The other subjects covered in these chapters include ritual magic, esoteric witchcraft, and the ancient art of divination and physiognomy.*

The Way of Heaven and Earth

天道地動之習

Tendo Chido no Narai

An example of misdirection on a smaller scale is when a stage illusionist subconsciously forces you to look in one direction so that you will not see them doing a certain activity in another. Here we see that the shinobi had to use the technique of misdirection on many levels, from constructing situations that would distract people while he went about his business, to using the force of the natural weather to hide his actions.

Importantly, there is a reference in this chapter that shatters one of the myths that floats in the sea of misunderstanding about the fabled ninja. In the ninja lore of the West there is a mistaken belief that the ninja will sacrifice his life and limb to fulfill his mission. This is similar to our impression of the suicidal tendencies of today's terrorists. The truth is far from that, as Natori writes about how the shinobi is very interested in staying alive, even at the cost of a mission's success. That is, a ninja should not attempt a covert activity until they had absolute confidence in their chances of success.

Tendo chido means to display tricks in the sky or construct strange or distracting things on the ground. This is done to attract people's attention either upwards or downwards and away from where you need to be. This is a method you are supposed to master to a high level.

Generally, when you need to circumvent or break through a fence or a wall, you should construct a strange object and place it at a high vantage point. That way, when people are coming and going along the street they the will focus their attention upwards and miss anything that is going on below them. If you need to cross over a fence and climb onto a clay wall, put something strange down on the street or under the wall on the opposite side of the road. The purpose of this is to create misdirection downwards and in the opposite direction from your activity.

Tendo means examining the *chi* of the sky and earth.

If there is anything you are concerned about in relationship to your covert activities, such as the wind, the rain, the sun, the moon, or the time, then you should always put off carrying out your plan and your mission. If you want to do well, then you should remember that a good shinobi would not commence a covert activity until everything sits well within his mind. However, there is hardly any precise way to predict anything before a said natural phenomenon takes place. There seems no way to decide on the right time of such things, unless you are extremely skilled at meteorology. How well the ancient masters did that, we can only make guesses.

The ancient Chinese divided the 283 constellations into 28 mansions. The mansions are latitudes the moon crosses during its monthly journey around Earth and they all have names. It is said it's always windy when the moon crosses the mansion lines of the following:

1. *Ki* 箕 the Winnowing Basket
2. *Heki* 壁 the Wall
3. *Yoku* 翼 the Wings
4. *Shin* 軫 the Chariot

Also, according to tradition, when a candle flame makes noises, you should be aware that it will become windy. Or when the candlelight emits more soot, it tells us that it's going to rain soon.

It will be rainy within three days when:

1. You see a great morning glow
2. The sun or the moon is partially clouded over

However, when the sunset is bright, the weather will be fine.

Other than these, there are various ways to predict the comings of the winds or the rains but most are unreliable, therefore, the details are not discussed here in any length.

Still, there is a tradition saying that all your concerns should be cleared away before you move into action. If you are annoyed with any of your concerns, then be aware you shouldn't perform your mission at all. Most people would like rainy nights, because it helps covert operations go more smoothly. However, remember, it would not necessarily be better to conduct your shinobi missions at night than during daytime; this is of course dependent on the place, situation and the time. Sometimes it so happens that the daytime would be better, so it is difficult to tell you when is the best time.

How to Get Over a High Place and Get in Through a Low Barrier

高越下キに入ルの習

Takaki wo Koe Hikuki ni Hairu no Narai

Disappearing in the middle of the night, escaping detection from an enemy is another stereotypical vision of the ninja that has merit based on this passage. We see from this chapter that the field agent would have been in close proximity to the "enemy" and would need to have a variety of tricks to get down from a height or escape through a hedge or a wall. This reaffirms the idea of the ninja leaping from castle walls or using his grappling hook to scale or descend enemy fortifications. However, it does show that, like all humans, they are limited in their ability by the physical limitations that rule us all. Natori viewed these limitations as challenges for the ingenuity of the shinobi, and so using their creativity would help them circumvent any obstacle.

This chapter is about tools.

Though there are various tools that a shinobi should have, if you have those tools or equipment and they are particularly strange or look out of place for the situation that you are in, they can arouse someone's suspicion. In a perfect world, you shouldn't carry any tools at all; even a tiny object like a needle might fall out when you have to move fast and give you away if the context is not right. You should be aware that such a single small thing could possibly unmask your cover as a shinobi soldier.

To climb a high wall or place, use a *kaginawa* grappling iron. If you put bamboo cylinders on the *kaginawa* rope and use a coin as a washer in-between the cylinders you can make a rod if you pull the rope tight. You can use this to get over a wall when you have no other way to get a grip.

When you are descending from a height, you should use a length of bamboo or a spear as a stick to lean against the wall. In this way you can slide down the wall on your back to help you break the fall. Also, leaping down with a stick that is your own height, letting the stick land first and act as a buffer. Even if you fall down, it will still enable a lighter landing. Climbing up with a long or short sword is mentioned previously. This is where you use the sword as a footrest by leaning it against the wall. Be sure to tie the sword's long *sageo* cord onto your foot, otherwise you will not be able to pull it back up after you and you will lose your sword.

To get down from a height, you should use a prepared rope if you have one at hand. If you don't have one, undress yourself and tie up your clothing to make a temporary rope. If you are going to get down from a 3 *ken* 間 (18 feet, or nearly 5.5 m) height with a rope that is only 2 *ken* (12 feet, or nearly 4 m) in length, take heart; it is comparable to you jumping from only a 1 *ken* height. You should keep this in mind, this works in all situations no matter how far up you are.

In case you need to slip in through a window or skylight, you should remember the following: Japanese skylights that are left open all night are difficult to break in to as they have shutters on the inside of the wall. On the other hand, those windows that are shut every night are easy to break into as they don't have inside shutters in place and you can unlock the lock that is at the top and pull it down to allow you to enter the property.

There is a tool called a *tsuijiyaburi* 築地破り, this is a tool for breaking through clay walls. The overall length is 1 *shaku* 尺and 5 or 6 *sun* 寸 (about 18 inches, or 45–48 cm) long. It has a saw edge around the rim. You can use this to break through a wall by cutting while rotating it until you reach the other side.

If you need to get through a hedge, you can use a wooden tub with its bottom cut out making a hollow cylinder. Push it into the hedge to create a "hole" and make sure you can get through it. Then you'll need to make it ready for use for when you come back and wish to escape. Also, it is an easy way out if guards are chasing you. Make sure to take it out after you have passed through it. The reason for this is so that the enemy can't find the way out and will have trouble getting through the hedge, allowing you to escape unhindered.

To open sliding doors or paper screens, if they are latched from the inside then a *koshikoro* 小鋸 saw is the best thing to use.

When there is a lock or a latch, saw through the door or screen so that you can get your hand through it and unlock the screen from the inside. Remember this lesson, when you lock your own door from inside you should lock it in the middle and double up the fastening for greater protection against such similar tricks.

If you hear that there is a possibility that someone targeted you and will creep into your room while you sleep, then you should follow the next plan; Close all the doors in the room, but leave one with the latch undone and slightly ajar to tempt the intruder to use it. Next, hook a string to the middle of the door and then stretch it and attach it to your pillow or your topknot and then sleep tight without worry. If someone opens the door then the string will be pulled on, waking you in the process. It is often the case that an unskilled man may try to wait up all night to catch the intruder. This shows that he has no experience in these matters. If the enemy avoids breaking in the night that you stay awake and puts it off for two or three consecutive nights in a row,

Natori Masazumi's death certificate

The grave of Natori Masazumi

you will become worn out from sleep exhaustion and will eventually fall asleep in the end. As a consequence of this sleep deprivation, once you fall asleep in this state it is very hard to become alert immediately upon waking. This is more so at the onset of your sleep cycle, it is easy for the enemy to penetrate and creep in with stealth. Therefore, you should make sure to keep your body from exhaustion and stay relaxed.

In ancient times, there was a skill attempted by shinobi, or *yato* as they were known in old times, this is where they created a dummy and set it up in the position of a man. It is an interesting method, but it's not used, nor is it effective any more, because it needs to be done unnoticed, which is a very difficult thing to achieve. You should be aware that you shouldn't use any of the ancient ways that are known to people because you will lose the edge of surprise.

Changing Your Approach to the Shinobi Ways

忍ニ色を替ルと云習

Shinobi ni Iro wo Kaeru to Iu Narai

The programming of the mind is evident in all cultures, from shaking an outstretched hand in greeting to waiting in a line. Upbringing and social interaction trains us from a young age to act in a specific way in a social setting. For a ninja to fall into this trap of conforming to the norms shows the limitations of his skill. Natori urges his students to break those boundaries and to look beyond the norm and think unconventionally. In today's capitalist world, we often see unconventional thinkers as entrepreneurs, but in the day of the ninja this could mean the difference between success and failure on a completely different level. Also, like the business entrepreneur, the shinobi must keep his cards close to his chest, and examine the enemy's resources.

This chapter is about devising deceptions when you are on a covert activity—this is an important lesson that you should master.

It is interesting and useful for a shinobi to imply interest in one area while in actual fact they focus on another area. In other words, make your intended target pay attention to one direction through misdirection, and then to take advantage of his confusion. There are other similar methods, such as pretending to go northward while in fact heading south. Or you can draw people's attention to somewhere far away, to allow you to go about your mission nearby.

A Story

A *shi* 師, or master, told his good disciples to steal a large pot from a shop. However, they couldn't steal such a huge bottle during the daytime without getting caught. Then the master showed them how to take it in a true shinobi fashion. He went to the shop and simply purchased it. All his disciples laughed to see this. The master said the following about this lesson "That's exactly why you are not skilled. Your intention was to take the bottle directly, which makes you see nothing but the object itself. I first stole ten or so small drinking cups within my reach and hid them within my sleeves, I did this earlier on in the day. I got enough money by selling them that I bought the jar with that money, thus I stole the jar. This is how to change your approach."

Sometimes you have to gain information about someone's income and know how much money someone has. To explore this you should prepare an alluring object and offer for him to buy it for 2 or 3 *ryo* 両* saying that it is worth 10 *ryo* at least. Your target should then hope to obtain it of course, but if he doesn't have enough money at his command for such an object, he would not even try to get the money and cease to show interest in the object. If he can afford to get a loan, he will say that he can borrow money to pay for it and give it to you soon. By observing the way your target reacts, you can know exactly how much money

---

* A unit of currency. Though exchange rates fluctuated, 1 ryo was approximately worth the amount of rice that one person consumed during a year.

he has at his disposal. Therefore, you should remember this in case someone tries the same trick on you. If someone offers you a thing like this for sale, you should tell him you have an acquaintance who wants to get it and you can serve as an intermediary, not letting him know that you want to buy it for yourself and thus he has no information on you.

To get to know how many people there are in a target's retinue, you should insert an *ana'ushi* 牢人 or undercover agent*, and have them work in the household to get the information you require. In this way you could get information on the master's preferences and other valuable information. Pay careful attention to every possibility that arises before you.

---

* This term can also possibly be read as "ronin," and is possibly a play on words between the two interpretations.

Defending Yourself Against the Enemy

敵防キと云習

Tekifusegi to Iu Narai

This next chapter is a brief but expansive look into the reality of being a ninja, a glimpse at the world that for so long was hidden from us. Again Natori shatters our view of the ninja by stating that a ninja should not sacrifice his life at any time if he can avoid it. It is completely naive of us to perpetuate the stereotypical idea of a ninja cavalierly throwing away his life. Like the knights of medieval Europe, a ninja would have been a very expensive commodity to retain. The cost in training a full-fledged shinobi soldier must have been vast indeed and to simply dispose of them would have been foolhardy. Here we see the true nature of the shinobi and the value for his life.

What we do have in this section is confirmation of the stereotype that the ninja was not only dishonorable, but also encouraged to be so. Unlike the samurai, who, like the medieval knight, has a code of honor, the ninja was spared such restrictions. Natori teaches his students that it is not only acceptable for a shinobi to behave dishonorably, but that it is almost unavoidable.

An even more stereotypical trait of the ninja is displayed here, which is the ability to use covert activities to steal into a samurai home and steal his pair of swords to render him less lethal, or to destroy the enemy's arsenal to "take the teeth out of the bear," so to speak.

The last colorful glimpse you'll get is one that tends to be ignored or diminished: homosexuality in the warrior culture. Like the famed warriors of Sparta, homosexuality helped to create bonds of love between soldiers. The same is also apparent in shudo *"the love of the young" in the samurai class and their acceptance of homosexuality as a part of their culture. It is very interesting to see what Natori says about using sex to get what you want, and while this might hint at the subject of homosexuality, it could also be a reference to supplying prostitution, but we simply do not know.*

What a shinobi is meant to do is fulfill their mission without losing their life. Those ninja who can succeed on a mission are, in the end, described as good shinobi, even if they sometimes get behind schedule or hesitate.

If the target gets angry with you about something, it is best if you lay the blame on another person and walk away as soon as possible to diffuse the situation. Common sense tells you that it is a form of dishonorable behavior to pin the blame for what you have done on someone else, a shinobi shouldn't feel that way and should not regard it as disgraceful at all.

One of the jobs of a shinobi is to get at the enemy's long and short swords, taking them away before a confrontation. Also, you can hamper the enemy by taking other measures, such as damaging or removing the blades or breaking the spearheads, this is also an option for a ninja. All such things are the arts of the shinobi.

You can ply someone with booze, sex, pleasure, or gambling for the purpose of taking him in and getting your way. As you will be included in those pleasures, you must keep control of your mind and be sure not to lose yourself or your self-control.

Charms and Secret Rituals That Protect You from Being Targeted by the Enemy's Agents

代人に覘 ざる秘法の守り

Dainin Ni Nerawarezaru Hiho no Mamori

This subject matter is possibly the most complex to digest as a modern reader; it is the subject of witchcraft and sorcery. Before we enter this realm you must look at what is happening in the world at this time. The West was just coming out of the medieval age, America was a small outpost at the end of the world and most of the rest of the world was unexplored. Thus, witchcraft and charms were the norm in those times of religion, superstition, and exploration. This is not the place to fully discuss the concept of ritual magic, but it gives us further insight into the reality of the ninja and, from a romantic point of view, it puts the mystery back into this dark world that has been exposed by the light of modern research. Additionally, there is an amazing story of the master of a house who knows that his guest is a ninja and so he tries to poison him; in turn the ninja knows that the master is trying to poison him, and all the while this life-and-death drama is being hidden from the other guests of the household.

A more intricate and amazing piece of the ninja puzzle comes in the form of one of the spells Natori uses. The ninja enthusiast will be familiar with the art of kuji-kiri *or "nine cuts," contained within esoteric Buddhism. The use of this system is misunderstood, but there is one element that runs throughout all theories and that consists of a "grid form" that is cut into the air with the fingers held like a sword. This grid consists of five horizontal lines and four vertical ones and is used as a form of a protective barrier against evil will. It is interesting to note that this grid is used during one of the spells in this chapter, adding to the depth of mystery that surrounds the* kuji-kiri.

The spell on the right is a charm for protection: cut some coarse and heavy straw *bafunshi* paper into a 7 *sun* (about 8.25 inches, or 21 cm) square and write the spell on it. Paste it in the corner of the room you sleep in, in a southeast direction called *tatsumi* 巽. Also, you should bless it by performing cold water ablutions and fasting, making sure that you always carry it with you as a charm. This is a great secret ritual used by the shinobi.*

The spell on page 116 is a charm that makes people stick together or split up.

[Top left side of the ritual]
Date†

[Bottom left side of the ritual]
Write your name here‡
Write your opponent's name here§

[The notes written below the spell¶]

If you write down the spell without any space between the characters, you and the opponent will get along well. However, if you write the characters separately, setting a space between them, the two of you will have a falling out.

This is how to use this spell:

When you chant the names of the intended people of the spell, you fold the paper so that the two names overlap exactly, that means that the two of you will be on good terms. To create an argument

---

* The first two ideograms are unknown, however the last five ideograms are a common collection found in spells. They are pronounced "kyukyunyoritsuryo" and are believed to mean "may your wish come true soon."
† Top left set of characters in the illustration on page 116
‡ Bottom, second from the left set of characters in the illustration on page 116
§ Bottom left set of characters in the illustration on page 116
¶ The three columns of characters on the bottom right of the illustration on page 116

between two people with the same charm you have to fold the paper as above but so that the names do not overlap this time. This will result in an argument.

Also, if you prepare this same charm and place it within the folds of your kimono and then see the intended person, he or she will greet you warmly even if they do not usually have a good rapport with you at all. You could also cause a discord between the enemy and his retainers this way by using the spell in the negative way described previously. Additionally, you could fix a marriage by the means of this spell. It has many uses.

From ancient times, there are *fujonichi** 不定日 unlucky days, these are days you shouldn't ask others anything.

The unlucky days of the lunar month and associated times are as follows:

1st	All day
4th	At night
8th	Daytime
18th	At night
25th	Daytime
29th	At night

---

* Also is written as 不成日 or 不成就日, which are said to be days of bad luck when you can't succeed in anything, in accordance with the *Onmyodo* 陰陽道, traditional Japanese esoteric cosmology. Note that these dates are not based on the Western calendar but the Chinese version of 12 months with 29 or 30 days in each.

A Charm that Protects You from Being Injured While Having a Fight With an Enemy*

舎　　　　　　　下　　　暈　　　中　　　暈　　　上
屍　　　　　　　咒　　　鍠　　　咒　　　鍠　　　咒
龍　　　　　　　法　　　品　　　法　　　品　　　法
罪　　　　　　　　　　　軍　　　　　　　軍
団　　　　　　　　　　　噫　　　　　　　噫
噫　　　　　　　　　　　急　　　　　　　急
急　　　　　　　　　　　如　　　　　　　如
如　　　　　　　　　　　律　　　　　　　律
律　　　　　　　　　　　令　　　　　　　令
令

* It is of note to see in this "magical" script that it uses the six- and five-pointed star, common symbols of Western magic traditions. However, the pentagram here indicates the five basic elements in *Onmyodo*.

An explanation of the spell:*

Joryakuho 上略法: Upper Strategy [right hand grouping]

Churyakuho 中略法: Middle Strategy [center grouping]

Geryakuho 下略法: Lower Strategy [left hand grouping]

Write these spells in *shu* 朱 (vermilion red) with your own blood mixed into the ink; write them on a *shu*-colored *nishiki* 錦, a silk–gold embroidered cloth, and wear it on your chest when you go on any mission. Then, even if you fight against a mountain of swords, you will not be hurt. Fear not! This also serves as the so-called *yat-agai* 矢違い charms, charms that protect you from arrows.

Though there are lots of other charms, much more than the aforementioned, they are so murky and untrustworthy that many people do not use them. Some people say that those who rely on charms and spells and use this kind of sorcery are no different from women or children, those who are easily deceived by *miko* 神子 shrine mediums, the mysterious *yamabushi* 山伏, and so on. However, it is not appropriate to simply discard any of them. The reason for this is simple: there is no benefit in the defiance of regular habits that may be powerful and misunderstood. On the other hand, you must be careful that you do not elevate any eso-teric belief to be all-powerful—you must keep your head about you. *Bushi* warriors like to wear good armor, not only to protect themselves from arrows, but also, so that they feel brave and are prepared to die immediately as a result of any fighting that they do; using these spells is similar to using quality armor.

---

* This spell is constructed of three sections, "upper strategy," "middle strategy," and "lower strategy." You may note that the middle section across all three lines are identical. This translates to, "May it be implemented as quickly as the statutes," a common phrase in esoteric Japanese "magic." The upper parts consist of a form of ideogram but their reading is not available to us as some of the kanji are not recorded within the Japanese language. The spells are said to be taken from the Chi-nese general Huang Shigong and are contained within Natori-Ryū's scroll *Gunbai Yōhō* in the *Book of Samurai* series.

Some More Tips

You can use black burnt frogspawn to blind people's eyes if you need to. Disperse this from the windward side and people will have bleary eyes if it gets into contact with their faces. You can even use this when you "creep in," you could apply it on the eyes of those sleeping in the house. Even if you disturb them and they awaken, their eyes will be bleary and you will have the advantage.

Be sure to keep the following in mind in case others try to poison you. If you are working together with your allies or in a ninja team, you should be single-minded enough so that none of you eat anything that is offered to you while you are a guest of an intended target, they may know that you are a shinobi. The most important thing for you is not to eat anything intended just for you. If someone tries to give you poison, he will mix it into booze, tea, food, hot water and so on. However, it has to be in something only you eat and never share with the master or his retainers, it has to be a personal dish just for you. From ancient times there have been cases where the master poisons his guests; however, it is possible to give the poison back to the master of the house by stealthy methods. Keep in mind that there are countless ways to poison people via food, for example, changing the cakes that you are served for another one in the hope that the enemy will be poisoned.

You could recruit a spy on the spot in an ad hoc fashion if the need arises. If you go to someone's mansion and suspect that something strange is going on, talk convincingly to their children or to a male or female servant and ply them with some money, as a bribe will help you discover what you wish. If you tell them something likely about their parents, or relatives, something that they would not know about and then at the same time carefully bribe them with money, they will believe you easily and blurt out some important information that may confirm your suspicions.

Sheltering Under Trees

木陰之大事

Kokage no Daiji

We often see the ninja disappear into the night but no one ever asks the question, where does he go? Of course, a ninja feels the cold as we do and needs somewhere to sleep, that place might be in the dark of the forest, on a secluded mountain, or even in the pleasure quarters. Even more interestingly, Natori provides us with a glimpse into the Japanese way of life at the time; the custom of seducing people's daughters. He does leave us with a very controversial statement, a statement that hangs in the stagnant air of our politically correct world...never trust women!

Sometimes you may have to spend a night under the trees where you cannot take advantage of full concealment as you are out in the open. A true master of the shinobi arts would naturally search for a hiding place without rushing around at dusk and without having anyone challenge his actions. It is a matter of shamefulness if you draw suspicion on yourself and to be sought out by the enemy—a good shinobi never acts suspiciously.

If only you could find someone who is willing to house you, even for one night, that would be a great help. In the case where you cannot find anyone, consider the pleasure quarters to be a fine alternative. This type of pleasure is something that people try to do without being seen, everybody has reason to hide their attendance at such places, even husbands, as they often go there in secret. Therefore, it should suit you for the purpose of concealment and no one will ask you questions.

After you wander from one place to another to collect information from people during the daytime, you should find shelter in such places as mentioned above to avoid suspicion. Alternatively, you could seduce someone's daughter; this will allow you to act better in your covert mission through the connection you have with her and her family. However, never forget that even if you have seven children with a woman, you shouldn't go and let your guard down when you are with her, as she cannot be trusted. This is a good warning, therefore, you should appreciate it.

The Art of Misdirection and Confusion

事を紛らかす之習

Koto wo Magirakasu no Narai

As we have seen, the ninja tried to master the art of misdirection as a skill. Now Natori is adding to that repertoire with the skill of misleading the detective or investigator. This chapter shows us that a ninja would take his time to understand how people would investigate his whereabouts, and he would try to keep one step ahead of them by planting false clues, leaving false evidence, and playing on people's need to brag. Thus, creating confusion and second guessing for the investigating team that was in hot pursuit of him.

Luck has a massive part to play in concealment and chance has a lot to do with whether you give yourself away or not. But remember that you could put yourself at risk of being uncovered if you talk to low-minded scum and take them into your company—be careful with whom you consort.

When you think that your cover will be revealed, you should create something strange or an incident somewhere else and divert people's attention to it. They will concentrate on the issue at hand and give you some time to recover. An example of this is when returning from a mission of stealth, a skilled shinobi would leave a tool or object that would create misdirection and confuse any investigation. This is a very clever method, as it is intended to make people investigate a false lead. Leaving a fake letter, tricking someone into creating something strange or making up false traces of you, anything that gives misleading information are methods that are all commonly used by a ninja to take people off his scent.

Some Tricks

Allow people to observe what you want them to, this will encourage people to disclose that information that you have supplied to them without being asked. They will do this voluntarily and act as a witness for your planted information. This is because people willingly talk about themselves or what they know out of egotism. It is vital for you to master this deception above all things. There are many similar ways to do this, but you should be creative according to the opportunity at hand. Further details needn't be given here, use your mind to its fullest. If a master shinobi plans anything, he should create the simplest method possible to achieve his goals and have the opponent make a serious mistake through straightforward traps. Therefore, make any plan so that it will be done as easily as possible without complications and have lightness to it. If you create something difficult, "heavy" and complex, it could cause people to be suspicious and as a result it may be investigated thoroughly, thus losing of the purpose of your deception. You should keep this firmly in mind.

How to Make People Tell You What They Think

人ニ理を盡くさする習之事

Hito ni Ri* wo Tsukusasuru Narai no Koto

Nobody takes notice of the village idiot and nobody cares what the stupid man does; also we have the phrase "loose lips sink ships." This was the basic protocol for a shinobi soldier. To quote Natori, "It is said that a well-trained shinobi looks like a very stupid man." If people do not understand your capabilities, then they will not fear you and they will let their guard down when you are around—a skill that must have been very useful for the shinobi. Another great lesson here is the command to continue to nourish our minds and learn all we can, for knowledge is true power.

---

* Two kinds of ideograms are used for the word "*Ri.*" One is 理, which means "reasons" and the other 利, which means "being sharp, quick, lucky, advantageous, etc."

This section is about the advantage of making people think that they are smarter than you are, with the aim to glean information indirectly from them. You should never divulge your true capabilities for any reason.

To make people reveal their opinions, you should pretend to be too stupid to think reasonably, and ask someone to tell you what they think about a certain subject you wish to know about. Then inflate their ego by giving them credit, saying things like: "That's true, it makes a lot of sense, you are correct." Then they will always be swellheaded and begin to boast about how intelligent they are and enjoy the conversation. If you then listen carefully, you could possibly get some hints or indications from them about the future plans or secrets that you are after.

If you have picked up on something and try to ask for further explanation, do not give out your reasoning or rationale to the opponent beforehand, you will not get anything else useful and you will be losing ground as they will become quiet on you. This is because people wish to show how intelligent they are and they want to see you as more stupid; therefore you should just disguise your own reasoning power and gain information through listening.

Part of a shinobi's skill set is to be careful and not show your true intelligence at any time. If you have aptitude inside of you, then you could, if you needed to, freely prove that you are indeed smart, but there is little need. It is really import for you to keep nourishing the concept of *dori*—your ability to reason.

A well-trained shinobi looks like a very stupid man. It is a core principle to praise others as much as possible to keep them carrying on about a subject at their own leisure, this skill is called *hito wo kuruma ni kakeru* 人を車にかける, it means "to get people carried away by praising them." You have to keep it in mind, as this is an invaluable lesson for a shinobi who wishes to gain information.

Reading Someone's Character by His Face

人相を知る事

Ninso wo Shiru Koto

This is the first of two chapters that are the most difficult for our modern minds to comprehend; at first glance you may see no connection between his writings and our modern world. For Natori, he judges people by their looks and appearance, whereas in a modern society, we are told that you can never judge a book by its cover. It is here that we really have to examine ourselves and not the medieval ninja. We all, each and every one of us, do judge people by their appearances, we just don't admit to it. If we see an obese person or an unattractive face, a person of another race or social class, we can find ourselves harboring a stereotype, even if just for a moment. Thus, we can see that Natori is asking here for you to understand that people's personalities can come from their features and to have an open mind as you examine each person and try to see them for who they are.

It is said that you can read what someone's natural character is just by looking at him or her; however, there are some doubts about this method. Still, the tradition says that if you look with a serene mind, it will reflect all, as clear as a mirror. However, when your mind is disturbed and not at peace, you may interpret a face incorrectly, so it will do more harm than good. It is fundamental for a shinobi to observe the opponent as carefully as possible and to get into their mind by trusting their trained instincts.

First, you must observe the person's posture, movements, voice, face color, and expressions. Within the face there is a name for every part, from your hairline all the way through your nose and to your chin.*

The five areas of the forehead divided from the top down.

Tenchu 天中 — Top part of the forehead

Tentei 天庭 — Upper part of the forehead below the *tenchu* above the *shiku*

Shiku 司空 — Upper middle part of the forehead below the *tentei* above the *chusei*

Chusei 中正 — Lower middle part of the forehead below the *shiku* above the *indo*

Indo 印堂 — The *glabella*, which is the space between the eyebrows and above the nose

Other Parts of the Face

Sankon 山ん根ん — The base of nose

Nenjo 年上 — The top of the nasal bone

JuJo 寿上 — The top of the nasal cartilage

JunTo 準頭 — The tip of the nose

Ninchu 人中 — The vertical line between the nose and the upper lip

Suisei 水星 — Mouth

Shojo 承漿 — Between the bottom lip and the chin

Chikaku 地閣 — The chin

---

* These names are also shared with acupuncture points.

Menso Santei 面相三停 **The Three Areas Within the Face**

Jotei 上停	From the hairline down to the eyebrows. If this is long, you will be happy in your old age
Chutei 中停	From the eyebrows to the tip of your nose. If this is long, you could be a king of men
Katei 下停	From the nose to the chin. If this is long, it means bad luck in most cases

People who have good features in all the three areas are considered to have a "lucky face." As for women, it is said to be almost the same as men. Yet, those women with a masculine voice, with a prominent uneven forehead and who are angry looking will have bad luck.

The Three Areas
of the Whole Body

怨体に三停ある事

Sotai ni Santei Aru Koto

This is the second chapter of Natori's discussion on physiognomy, the art of telling someone's character by their dimensions and features. Before we scoff at this skill and pass it off as medieval madness, we must realize that this was a profound and respected skill for over two thousand years, from ancient Greece to medieval Europe. With resurgences and declines, it has nearly always been a part of modern human culture. However, Natori confuses the issue more by mixing this ancient "science" with divination and fortune telling, to the point where the two are inseparable. This does make sense considering that science, magic, and religion were synonymous for the medieval mind. There are three things we can take from this: Firstly, that Natori has faith in a higher understanding and a sense of belief that penetrates his life; Secondly, that he is actively investigating what it means to be human, a topic of universal appeal and under continuous study and scrutiny; And lastly, that he has the modesty and sincerity to admit that he is no expert.

The top section of the head is called the *jotei* 上停. If you are a leader of people and have a large head, you will not be poor but also, you will not live long. A person with a small and elongated head will have bad luck for all his life. Also, those with shaking knees when sitting, having a small waist like a bee, and down-turned corners of the mouth are said to have dire luck in life.

The part from the shoulders to the hips is called *chutei* 中停. If the length of this area is short, you will die young or you will be evil-natured. If this area from the shoulders to the hips is shorter than legs, you are considered to be poor and mean. Those women with straight shoulders that have sharp edges have to wait for men as they don't have a matchmaker to get them a good marriage.

The part from the hips to the ankle is called *katei* 下停. If it is longer than the *chutei*, the shoulders to the hips, you will be sick a lot or will move to another province. When you laugh at others, covering your mouth with your hand, scratching your eyebrow or looking at them sideways, this is the sign of a prostitute. Also, those women who have a bony body are considered as being servants.

Those who have proper proportions within these three parts are considered to have good luck. If anything is too big, small, long, or short, it is called *shoakuso* 少悪相 the concept of slightly bad luck.

The *jotei* 上停 or top of the head.

This is called the *roppu* 六府, or "the six bones," which are the malar cheekbones, zygomatic bones (lower part of the eye socket and cheek bones), and the lower mandible. Those with these bones that can be seen from the surface, and are full-fleshed with no hollows and have a quite flat and smooth face are considered to have a lucky face. When walking, those walking with their bodies swinging and hips sticking out behind are considered mean-minded. People with wide nostril wings are considered to be mean and shabby.

Also, it is said there are signs of prosperity and long life, they are as follows and resemble Buddhist teachings:

1. A full-fleshed top of the head
2. A large belly when the back is relaxed
3. Red lips and white teeth
4. Round ears with thick earlobes
5. A straight ridge of the nose
6. Eyes with the black and white parts distinct. Beautifully arched and long eyebrows
7. Sloping shoulders with a flat and broad chest
8. A round and flopping belly
9. To be equally proportioned in these 3 areas, full-fleshed, bones with no contortions, long arms and/or long legs

Furthermore, the mouth should be like a halo,* the eyes should be clearly lighted, with the eyelids not drooping down, the face not frowning when looking at something. Gentle-looking eyes, but with the corner having the ability to be raised quickly when looking. Having wrinkles and clean skin of the face while having a dignified look even when not angry and to be calm and have a honorable presence. It is a positive characteristic to be like a big ship tossing on the waves, not upset even when angry, never losing the equilibrium of the mind even when in grief. Those who have all these features of the six bones of *roppu* are said to have a fortune and to live a rich, precious, happy, and long life.

Further propositions of a positive nature are:

Having a great voice that carries well; a clear mind; to be heavily boned; having a large forehead; thin inside ends of the eyebrows; being motionless while speaking; to look like a mountain when sitting, smelling good like orchids and the Japanese Judas tree.[†]

Also:

Ears that can't be seen when viewed head on; a long tongue;

---

* He writes it in *hiragana* as えんこう. it is considered to be 円光, which means a halo.

† *Cercis Siliquastrum.*

round-ended, thin and long fingers; hands that reach below the knees* when the arms are in a relaxed position at your side; having hair or a mole on the soles of the feet.† Those people with these features are destined to become a saint and could be the ruler of the world. It is also positive if the five features of eyes, ears, nose, mouth and chin are good looking, well-shaped, and clean. A resonant voice, good long breathing, no gaps between the teeth and a moistness of the mouth are needed for a good character. Navels should be so deep as to have the ability to hide the fruit of jujube, which means you need a deep navel. Bellies that are not so flat but pulling down. Smooth skin, patience in eating, a still neck when swallowing, these are also signs of good luck.

Indications of Long Life:

1. To be heavily bearded under the nose, having much hair inside of the ears and the nose
2. A refreshing, straightforward character
3. A fine bony framework, hard flesh, flexible muscles and resonant voice
4. To be tall, cheekbones close to the ears, big long ears having much hair inside them, long eyebrows with some gray hair
5. The *noko* 脳戸 point and the *chinkotu* 枕骨 occipital bone should have a good length
6. A moist palm, well-fleshed insteps, and to be happy-looking

All these are indications for long life.
On the other hand here are a few examples of signs of bad luck:

1. Those who look at others from under his brows and have protruding eyes will not have a good rapport with people
2. Eyes that are hidden when laughing
3. A grimy face, with many moles
4. A deep and gravel-like voice

---

* This seemingly impossible trait is also a Buddhist trait.
† The last two here seem like strange ideas because they do not appear in the Buddhist scriptures.

5. Irregular teeth
6. For the pinna (the fleshy extremes of the ears) to not have some forward curl
7. A thick head of short hair

These are signs of bad luck that will be with you all through life.

Those who don't wake quickly, with their body becoming cold like ice when in sleep, are shabby in nature.

Those who have a mole between their eyebrows are humble to others. The shaking of knees and rubbing of the face while bowing the head are indications of adultery in women. Such women seek for illicit relationships or another marriage with other men outside of the marital bed.

The Parts of the Body

The Head

If the forehead is boxy in nature and has "corners" on both sides, with the bones behind the ears being protuberant, like horns, which are named *jukotsu* 寿骨, indicate a long life. A round-shaped head, of short length, is a sign of wealth and high rank. White hair, but black in the back of head, indicates excellent luck. A round upper head or boxy-shaped head that feels moist also denotes good luck. Black thin hair means prosperity if one gets into office. Thick and long hair* indicates bad luck. A low hairline on the nape of the neck is also a bad sign. Those with low hair that whorls down to the nape are said to be suspicious.

The Eyebrows

Thin, flat and moist ones are good. Long linear eyebrows are a sign of wisdom. Those who have a mole within the eyebrows are intelligent, wise, and wealthy. Those that are high on the forehead denote a high rank. Those who have white hair in the eyebrows

* Remembering that Natori's version of long hair may be different to modern terms as most had the traditional topknot due to their rank.

are of a long-life. Those who have a longitudinal wrinkle above eyebrows are wealthy. Those with moist eyebrows are wise and intelligent. Long eyebrows, extending past the eyes means honesty and faithfulness. Those with straight horizontal eyebrows have loyalty to their master. It is also said that a narrow region of the *glabella*, (the area between the eyebrows) and a standing out of the superciliary bones of the eyebrows are signs of bad luck. Those with scanty eyebrows lie and those with slanted eyebrows are weak natured.

The Eyes

Long, deep, glaring, and moist eyes are the indication of an exalted personage. Black,[*] shiny, lacquer-like eyes denote the wise, quick-witted, and scholarly attained. Thin and deep eyes are a sign of long life. Those who have birthmarks on both bottom lids are blessed in clothing and food. If the bottoms of both eyes align on a straight line, it is said to be a sign of a lord of a province. Triangle or corn-shaped eyes are of bad luck. Those with badly downward slanting eyes get divorced easily. Those with an upward glance are not faithful and steal.

The Nose

A tip of nose that is not uptilted but prominent enough is an indication of wealth and a long and happy life. Noses with no obvious characteristic are of good luck. The *jinchu* 人中, or *philtrum*, is the vertical groove below the nose. A deep, straight philtrum, not narrowing toward the lips but broadening in an A-shape indicates luck. If it is narrow on top and broad at the base, the person will have a lot of children and grandchildren. Those with straight ones have loyalty about them. U-shaped ones, like split bamboo, denote a high rank and wealth. Those with a mole on the top of the nose will have lots of sons, those with one on the base, daughters. Those with ones on both sides of it will have two children. Those with a horizontal line across the philtrum will have no children at all.

---

[*] There is no mention of foreign eyes, those being blue or green, as all Japanese people have dark eyes.

There are some people whose philtrums are very flat and scarcely have indentation. You should be aware that they will never have a child. Also it is said those who have a not-so-pointed tip of the nose are liars. Those with horizontal wrinkles on the nose will be involved in an accident caused by a horse and carriage. Those with a high-pointed and hooked nose will defeat others. Those with a scraggy nose will die in other provinces. Those with turned-up nostrils are so poor that they don't have food at home even for the night of their return.

The Ears

Thick, hard, long ears that are not flat in the shape of its upper part are desirable. A smooth outer ear, that is a smooth and round shaped auricle, with earlobes toward the mouth on a forward in-clination indicate wealth and long life. Those with a lot of hair inside the ears have the sign of a long life. Those with moles on the ears are wise, and will bear a child with a person of exalted rank. Wide ear canals indicate wisdom and discretion. Those whose contours of the ears and earlobes are thick and long, have righteousness and loyalty, and if educated, will be known to the whole world. Dirty and ill-shaped ears are of the stupid and poor. Those ears that are higher than the eyes, like a mouse, are poor. Those with turned-up ear canals, with no concavity, will become orphans. Those who have small ears and a big mouth are liars.

The Mouth

Square broad lips, which are a little high on the philtrum, are an indication of exalted personage and long life. Those with red lips shaped like a bow with a string will be high in official rank. Upper and bottom lips, which are broad in width, red and thick indicate good luck and having enough clothes and food. Those with a rectangular-shaped mouth have very good fortune and wealth. Those with thick lips and a thin tongue have good luck. Those with a thick tongue and clear voice are decent. If someone has deep red lips and his or her teeth can't be seen when he or she smiles, it is an indication of exalted personage. Those with thick upper and bottom lips are said to have loyalty. Also, it is said that sharp and turned-up lips indicate base indecency. Those who move their mouth even when they are not talking will die of hunger. Those with a mouth like a rat defame others and are quite envious. Those whose lips look like the action of blowing on a fire are poor. Those with a vertical line, like a dog, on the mouth will die of hunger.

The Teeth

Big, long, shiny teeth with no gaps indicate good fortune. Those teeth that are not protruding denote wealth and honor. You should be aware that those having 38 teeth are kings,* those with 36 are nobles and princes, 34 are men of wisdom, 32 happy, mean and wealthy, 30 ordinary and with good luck, and 28 base and mean. Those having teeth shaped like pomegranate seeds have good fortune, those with pointed teeth are high in rank, and those with teeth that are shaped like rice grains will have a long life. A red tongue and lips and white teeth indicate learned wisdom. Those with overlapping teeth are bad natured. Those with misaligned and irregular teeth are liars.

The Tongue

Properly long tongues are of good luck. Those whose tongue reaches the nose when sticking it out will ascend the throne or become a lord, those with a hard and flat tongue are of an exalted personage. Those with a thin and long tongue lie. Those with a pointed and short tongue are greedy. Tongues with different colors are a bad sign.

The Hands

Those with slender hands are benevolent and generous. If the hands reach below the knees when the arms are in a relaxed position at the sides, the person is wise. Those who have a small build

---

* The total number of an adult's teeth is 32, so the numbers 38, 36, or 34 are impossible and only imaginary.

and big hands have good luck and wealth. Thick hands have the connotation of wealth and nobility. Those having thin and long fingers are intelligent. Those having a thick and long palm are also of an exalted personage. Palms that are thick outward and hollow inward indicate wealth and nobility. Those whose palms are red will be prosperous and successful. Those having a mole on the palms are wealthy and noble. Thin and deep lines of the palm indicate good luck. A straight vertical line on the palm is a good sign. If the line reaches even onto the finger, the person will realize his heart's desire in everything. Those with many thin lines like a mass of tangled threads on the palm are bright and intelligent. Those with snail-like whorls for fingerprints on all ten fingers and thumbs will reach their height of glory. Thick nails are desirable. In general, those with moist and smooth nails have wisdom.

Also, short and thick hands indicate baseness and greed. Those whose hands don't reach the hips when the arms are in a relaxed position are ungraceful and mean all of their lives. Those who are of large build and have small hands live in honest poverty, poor but not greedy, so that they will get pleasure out of their lives. Those with smelly and sweaty palms are poor and mean.

The Lines of the Palm

Hated and Undesirable Lines of the Palm

Having the following lines on the palm of people's hands are signs of negativity.

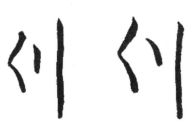

断頭紋 *Dantomon*
(Lines of beheading)

横死紋 *Oshimon*
(Lines of unnatural death)

刀字 *Toji* (The letter 刀"sword")

丁字 *Teiji* (The letter T)

枷鎖紋 *Kasanomon* (*Cangue*)*

---

* A device for public humiliation not dissimilar to the stocks of Europe.

夜叉紋 *Yashamon* (Demon)

火字 *Hinoji* (The letter 火 "fire")

土字 *Tsuchinoji* (The letter 土 "soil")

産死紋 *Sanshimon* (Death of a child)

妬妻紋 *Tosaimon* (Jealous wife)

Lines of Decency, Wealth and Wisdom
People with these lines will have great
achievement.

柳絲紋 *Ryushimon*
(Long branches of a willow tree)

三爻紋 *Sansamon* (Triple letters 乂)

One letter of 乂

縄紋 *Jomon* (Rope pattern)

生魚 *Seigyo* (Fresh fish)

華蓋 *Kakai* (Flowery cover)

金井 *Kanai* (Golden well)

双井 *Sosei* (Double letter" 井")

三井 *Sansei* (Triple letter "井")

19 一文紋* *Ichimonmon*
(The letter "一")

金印 *Kin'in* (Gold seal)

棋盤 *Kiban* (Japanese chessboard)

穿銭 *Sentsu* (Perforated coins)

Moles

It is said that those with moles that can be seen are not very lucky, while those with hidden ones indicate good luck.

Those who have a mole on the *indo* 印堂, the space between the eyebrows, are noble and wise. Those having one on *sasho* 左廂, the upper left side of the forehead, will rise to a high rank, or become very wealthy but will live away from their parents from an early age. The left of the *tenchu* 天中, center top of the forehead is called the *tengaku* 天岳. The left of *tengaku* is called the *sasho*.

---

* It seems to be a mistake. Assumingly he meant the letter "十".

A mole on the sole of the foot indicates high rank or wealth and those with a mole on the thigh attend to a person of high rank. Those having one on the left underarm will be successful if they hold a public office. Those with one below the navel are wise and wealthy.

If any other color of a mole is mixed with red or black, it is a sign of bad luck. A mole at the corner of the eyes denotes being evil natured or of thieves. Those with a mole at the corner of the eyes will be killed by an arrow. If you have one on your left side, you will be drowned. Those who have ones in line on the right and left sides of the ears will be disabled. If you have one on the *jinchu* 人中 philtrum, it is classed as not desirable because you are considered to be single.

If you try to learn to read people's characters by physiognomy be warned that it is difficult and there is no way of mentioning every detail of it. Only the outline is written here because physiognomy isn't always right nor has come true since ancient times. For instance, in case that one person has a very undesirable feature while having a very lucky one as well, there is no problem with the fact that they go together. If you try to tell someone's fortune exactly, by balancing out good and bad, you should consider the details carefully but be warned it still does not always come true. If you concentrate yourself like this, you will try every effort to know the opponent's intention. However, trying too hard to read from his or her facial features, you may end up staring at his or her face without taking your eyes off them, even for a moment—it would be extremely discourteous and you shouldn't do that.

Be aware that you should make a concentrated effort to know the opponent's mind so that you can use the information for your shinobi activities.

This is the end of the middle chapters.

PART FOUR

The Shoninki Final Chapters

正忍記下巻

Shoninki Ge Kan

The final set of chapters of the Shoninki *deals with what we can use in our day-to-day lives: The philosophy of the shinobi, and their undisputed discipline and courage. It deals with conversational studies, psychology, keeping your wits about you when you are under stress, and learning how to be a dignified and true warrior who sticks to the shinobi codes created by the ancient masters.*

Secret Philosophies

極秘傳

Gokuhiden*

Natori here is introducing the final chapters and setting the stage for the lessons to come. He is preparing the reader to expand on their thinking and to explore the possibilities and realities of the human mind and what it can achieve. As interesting as any of the samurai treatises (remembering that Natori was in fact a samurai), this insight into the mind of the ninja is an unbelievable opportunity for any true martial artist to understand more deeply the path of bushido.

---

* *Gokuhiden,* literally "the tradition of complete secrecy."

Although there are millions of lessons for the shinobi that are both subtle and ever changing, you can't teach them in their entirety by tradition or passing them on. One of the most important things for you to do is always try to know everything you can of every place or province that it is possible to know. When you are in that said province, you will be able to read the feeling of the local people and do what is necessary according to the situation. If your mind is in total accordance with the way of things and it is working with perfect reason and logic, then you can pass through the *mumon no ikkan* 無門の一関 "the gateless gate." This is the interface with humans and is the gateway to their true thoughts through observing them. You will be able to pass through this mental stage because you will have a clear mind and reasonable thinking due to your training.

You shouldn't try to point out or comprehend what morals and honors the human mind could achieve under all the eternal possibilities of existence. If you did, it would be spread as widely as *rikugo* 六合, the whole universe, that is the four cardinal directions and the two directions of above and below. On the other hand, it is amazing that if you write the categories of the human mind onto scrolls, it would fit into a very limited space.* The human mind is marvelous and flexible. It's amazing. As time goes by, clearly or mysteriously, you will realize the essence of things and understanding will appear to you from nowhere. You may wonder what has made things thus. On this, you should master everything and all that you can.

The traditional philosophies written in these final chapters are the requirements you need to understand in order for you to master the esoteric path of the shinobi. Because the written word is not a perfect representation of verbal communication, and verbal communication is not a perfect representation of human thought, you should use your imagination and insight to realize and grasp the way of all matters.

---

* This paradoxical statement is not only hinting at the complexities of the mind and its vastness, but also the ability to catalog and label vast areas under a small selection of titles.

The Gateless Gate

無門の一関

Mumon no Ikkan*

Preparation and a firm mindset are the lessons given in this section. To be prepared in all you do and to have a relaxed and steady personality are the keys to success for the shinobi. Surprisingly, this chapter is probably closest to the reality of most of the ninja's work. We can conclude that a ninja was an information gatherer, spy, and scout most of the time, and this is his secret to success. In this section, Natori shows one how to gather that information, how to prepare the subject for subtle investigation and how to make them divulge the secrets that they have. With a warning that your mind must be as sharp as a knife and that you should excel in mental capabilities to keep ahead of your peers, this set of lessons is one we can carry forward into our own lives with ease.

---

* Literally, "checkpoint without a gate." Quoted from *The Gateless Gate*, a collections of Zen koans complied by the Chinese Zen Master, Wumen Hui-k'ai 無門慧開 (1183–1260). "The gateless gate" is considered to have a double meaning. One is "checkpoint having no gateway through which to pass," and the other is "that having no barrier to block your path." In Natori-Ryu, *mumon no ikkan* is the concept of passing through the interface of a human to discover their true thoughts.

Nothing is more difficult than to read other people's minds. The more you try to make someone talk about one thing, the more they will conceal it from you. Therefore, the first thing you should do is to carry conversation along other lines, then you can draw out what you need by making him feel bloated with a sense of his own superiority and intelligence. You should strive to get any hint of what you need within his words and not miss a thing by taking it all in.

If he is concealing something skillfully, treat this as suspicious and that he has something of importance to hide. In such a case, focus on this and keep trying to draw it out of him for as long as possible, but don't be in a rush, taking a relaxed approach and biding your time will reward you in the end.

Hence, when others are eagerly asking you questions, you should just say things you don't mean, trying to fathom their intention and discover if they are probing you for information. There is a good old proverb, which says:

"One who asks will not slip, one who speaks will give out."

This holds true. Try to make them keep talking about similar topics to the one that you are investigating. Anything that looks unnatural should be avoided as to not arouse their suspicions.

To know if someone is an enemy's spy, you should observe and fathom his intentions first. If he is eager to ask for what seems to have nothing to do with him, or if he talks too logically for his characteristics, be aware that he must have been told to do so by someone else and thus he is a spy. In the case that his conversation is based on these borrowed opinions, then you should change the topic of the conversation, this way he will get confused and he cannot be consistent in his words and avenues of investigation.

A good shinobi can penetrate another person's mind without letting them know that they have been penetrated. The ninja can pass through the mental state of the *mumon no ikkan* "checkpoint" without his intentions being recognized, this is indeed a terrifying skill to have. To deal with people, you should completely master the skill of this school mentioned before called *kuruma ni kakuru* 車にかくる, this is the skill of flattery to gain knowledge.

By using this technique, you can steal into the opponent's mind with great ease without drawing his attention in a way to make him wary, meanwhile he bleeds all the information that you need—truly amazing.

If you try to get someone in your clutches when you have not prepared yourself and you are not in the correct state of mind, it will always be noticed and you will be deceived as a result. Just try to be resourceful at all times and use the capacity of your imagination fully on the opponent. As soon as you find a gap in your enemy's defenses, take it quickly...then you will succeed.

Here is an old verse:

> *"As a matter of course you may be certain of your victory with the coming of dawn, but the moment you open the door, a ray of the moon will get in through it."*

This means you shouldn't let your guard down at any time.

How to Avoid Defeating Other People

人ヲ破らざる之習

Hito wo Yaburazaru no Narai

This lesson connects to the last chapter and is an extension of those teachings, but concentrates on a fundamental aspect; do not defeat your enemy. This seems almost paradoxical because it seems that the purpose of having an enemy is to defeat them. For the apprentice ninja, they must have had to learn to curb that instinct of wishing to win "points" over the enemy. For ninjas, much of their time was not encountering the enemy face-to-face with drawn swords, it was more of a duel with words. It is here that the ninja resembles politicians or modern police—using words and investigation techniques. Here we learn that once you offend or defeat someone, it is a hard climb back to the starting point and that they will be overly defensive towards you as a result. Thus, we learn to tread with care and to master our own lack of restraint.

If you psychologically defeat others, you will not be able to attain a desired result or get your needed information. If you offend them too much, they will lose their temper and get upset and become competitive, thus, your aim will not be achieved. Therefore, in information gathering, you should sometimes depress the opponent, or sometimes you should build them up, but it is hard to tell the slight nuances of difference, so keep your mind sharp.

Be aware that there are four principles to be used in conversation and each needs to be used in their appropriate place. The four principles are:

1. *Go* — Hard
2. *Kyo* — Strong
3. *Ju* — Flexible
4. *Jaku* — Weak

Those who don't know how to use them appropriately will be hard when they should be yielding or they will be strong when they should be weak, this is seemingly guided by some mysterious power of will and therefore you should be very sensitive about which application you use.

1. There is a method where you identify with your enemy, which means you should guess with your own mind what he is thinking or the angle he is using. As all things in the universe—such as the trinity of heaven, earth, and man—are common to us all, you will find that everyone is cold in winter and hot in summer, thus, when you are cold, so is the opponent. When you know a lot about a place, so may the opponent. Therefore, in this method you should know your enemy by using an analogy to yourself and preempting his moves.
2. There is another method where you "take" your enemy's mind. It is to guess accurately what results you will get if you set up a situation around him or what his response will be to your conversation. If you can achieve this desired result,

it could be said you have attained this skill of "the taking of the enemy's mind." How clever it is and what a godlike skill to have! It seems quite clear that this is superior to the above mentioned, "identifying with the enemy" as the enemy follows your expectations.

3. There is still one more method: This is where you disconnect from the enemy completely. In this method, you should behave independently; the enemy is the enemy— you both have different ways of reasoning and don't have much in common. Even using such a method, you can attain your goal without fail, which is nothing less than the art of true mastery. That is to say, there is no point in trying this skill and alienating yourself from the enemy unless you have attained a high level.

You can take advantage by using the opponent's words and attitude against him only when you have full confidence in your own work. Also, it is a subtle and difficult art to make him talk while placing distance between you and him and to not play along. This is such an art of conversation that would enable you to overwhelm even the strongest enemy or deceive even the smartest ones. This lesson should be greatly appreciated as it is most valuable. You should devote every effort to honing your skills on this path.

Reading People's Personalities*
心相之事
Shinso no Koto

In the world of psychology there has been a long ongoing debate regarding which has the greater effect on people, nature or nurture. Simply, this is the argument of whether humans are genetically inclined to have their given personality or if their environment (family, social, political structure) is the root of their personality. Most people are on the fence and many believe that both play a part in defining the human personality. However, there is an underlying issue: That a belief in nature as the most influential part of the human personality is indirectly accepting that humans have a soul and that this personality, at birth, had to be put there by something or someone. In the Buddhist world they had this belief centuries ago, while some Christians believe that God made you who you are—saint or sinner. The Buddhist idea is that everybody is given a set of the seven basic emotions, each one at a different level. The difference of levels in these emotions creates your fundamental character along with your upbringing and finally your self-analysis when you reach an age of wanting to improve yourself.

---

* The original title of this chapter is literally "About Mentality."

Thus, it seems that Natori and his school of ninjas were well ahead of their time in understanding the make-up of the human mind and the psychology that we are all still arguing about today. As a lesson, we should use his curriculum here to understand the faults of our own psyche and push ourselves to greater achievements.

This is an important technique; while studying the art of *ninso*—face reading—is about knowing a person from their looks and what we would call "instructional learning," this chapter is concerned with the art of *shinso* and is about gaining a deduction from a deeper analysis. Thus, with the art of *ninso*, you can be wrong. However with the art of *shinso*—the deduction of another's mind—you can count on this method to rarely fail and you will achieve the desired result.

First of all, you must observe your own mind as it is given to you by Heaven and see where it is out of balance. With this in mind, you should figure out where other people's minds are ill-proportioned.

Here is a list of fundamental and natural inclinations that each human has:

Delight: all people have an inborn inclination towards delight.
Anger: all people have an inborn inclination towards anger.
Sorrow: all people have an inborn inclination towards sorrow.
Pleasure: all people naturally seek pleasure and enjoyment in everything.
Love: all people have an inborn inclination towards love.
Evil: some people have a naturally darker mind.
Greed: all people have an inborn inclination towards greed.

The above are the seven emotions. In Buddhism, they refer to delight, anger, gloom, caring, sorrow, fear, and surprise—this is from the same concept and they are to be treated as one. No one is born with a complete balance of these seven emotions. If there is such a person, then they must be a saint. For a normal human these emotions keep changing as you mature and age. Thus, you are born with one predominant emotion and with this you later learn to carve out the other six, depending on your will.

A ninja can use this to their advantage because someone's true nature will usually come out and the other six will be set aside in the event of an emergency or urgent action—when all learning is put to the side, you see the core of a person. Each emotion comes in a countless number of ever changing ways. For instance, people will be delighted for many kinds of reasons, such as when they realize their desires, if they get promoted in official rank, or receive financial profit. However, you can't know the reason for their pleasure for sure unless they reveal it themselves.

People may get angry because they argue with others, or they incur loss, or they just blame the world for no reason. You can't tell exactly why they are angry. You only know that they are angry even if they don't verbally express it. So you must understand that even though the symptoms all look similar, the root causes could completely differ. This is like heaven and earth, this you should be aware of if you wish to manipulate people for your own purpose. There is still much information to be passed by word of mouth that cannot be written here.

Knowing the Difference Between the Righteous Path and Constructed Logic

道理と利口と知るべき事

Dori to Riko to Shirubeki Koto

Our modern world is filled with constructed logic, but we are lacking in reason and principle. Being clever is nice but lacks the depth that reason and principle hold. Being clever is about deceit, subterfuge and an ability to think quickly during an occurrence. Following the principle is about thoughtfulness, depth and wisdom. If only every single person in the martial arts world held this single lesson to heart, we would have a world of noble warriors to protect us from falsehoods and deception, a surprising and ironic lesson from a master ninja.

Primarily, the concept of *dori*—the righteous path—cannot be wrong but is something absolute; it will not transform, no matter when or what speech is used. In opposition to this is *riko*—constructed logic, this is interesting to hear but may go through transformation. *Honri*—true principle—is vast and extensive; when heard, it is humble and unpretentious but also explicit. Be warned, cleverness has no advantage over reason in any way but people would like to hear cleverness as it is pleasant to the ear and they will be attracted to its intelligence.

Figuratively speaking, the path of principle is like listening to a sound with your ears. You have little difficulty hearing sound even with a barrier in place. Constructed logic, on the other hand, is like seeing. Even with a simple piece of paper in front of you, you can't see through it and cleverness becomes useless. A good point about reason is it doesn't change even if transmitted over a million miles, while cleverness will not be as good as it once was when you heard it in person. Therefore, you should be aware that anything that changes easily is always cleverness and is not reason.

If you use *dori*—the path of principle—to see through situations but then use *riko*—constructed logic—in your plots to beguile people, while also keeping your true intentions covertly deep and hidden, then you will know that your conversation skills will automatically achieve wonders without any effort. However, if you talk with a half-hearted mind, the opponent will take advantage of you and your reason will be bent immediately, which will leave little possibility of your aim to be fulfilled. If that is the case, then you should be fully aware that you are under-skilled in this area.

Controlling Your Mind and Engaging with the Righteous Path

心之納理ニ當ル事

Kokoro no Osame Ri ni Ataru Koto

Miyamoto Musashi died in the seventeenth century, around the same time that the world of Natori was developing. It is of great interest that, in this chapter, we get the same insight into the samurai mindset as we get from reading the Book of Five Rings. This is a venture into the five basic elements of life and their connection to the mind. Natori emphasizes that you have to be able to cultivate your chi or "spirit" to be able to serve as a shinobi soldier and that you need to nourish your mind with pure thoughts and have the ability to transcend human needs and reach into that place where all martial artists journey: towards enlightenment.

To control your mind you shouldn't indulge your emotions or urges, but it is essential to strengthen your *chi*. Always try to restore your spirit, and do not waste it on unimportant things. It is essential to make your mind, spirit, and *chi* strong. Suppose you simply cannot achieve your aim, it might be because you lack energy and spirit. You should also be aware that if you neglect to nourish your true mind properly, you will run out of energy, get tired, and will end up failing at the last moment. You should also be aware that the faint-hearted cannot serve as shinobi no mono.

Generally, when you have inner peace, you can fathom things that other people don't realize and you can mentally outmaneuver people's thought processes without effort. If you can tolerate something intolerable or manage to refrain from advancing when the situation seems to urge you to do so and you know you should stop because you feel it inappropriate, then this is because of your strong spirit. You will need for nothing if your spirit is strong.

Nothing is as amazing as the human mind. It has the five phases*: wood, fire, earth, metal and water within it, and they can come out in rapid succession. However, it is the case that when you seek to find a specific one you generally cannot find it. Spirit can warm you up when cold, through breathing, even without a real fire, or it can cool you down without the aid of real water. This is a natural order of things. Wood resonates the voice, metal generates water, and earth generates metal.†
How marvelous the human mind is. The mind changes its form dependent on the vessel; similar to how water changes when it too is put into a vessel. Like fire that rages, the mind gains force and when a situation becomes advantageous to you. Wood grows, tall or short, according to its nature, spreading its roots for good balance. If the wind blows hard trying to fell a tree, the tree sways according to that movement. But if it fights back, it will break and snap in the wind.

---

* According to the Chinese theory of the Five Elements, each element has a selection of related emotions. Thus wood, fire, earth, metal and water all represent a state of emotion.
† This is based on the Creation Cycle of the Five Elements.

Though metal is hard, it forms itself in accordance to what people mold it into. Earth on the other hand brings forth reason through correlating to water, fire, wood and metal. Thus, the point is this: If you are not versed in this principle, your words will be empty and your skills will be awkward, so be firm in your reasoning and be like the elements when needed.

Impromptu Ways of Speaking

無計弁舌

Mukei Benzetsu

"Life is found in the way of death," is a famous samurai paraphrasing and one that is at the heart of the book, Hagakure *by Yamamoto Tsunetomo. This famous book was written in the eighteenth century and postdates the time of Natori Masatake. Thus, it is stunning to discover that Natori makes a similar statement and says that the way for the shinobi is that, "life exists within death, death exists within life." Essentially, we are told, if you seek to look for safety and a way out of danger, your mind is not keen and you will fail, thus losing your life. However, if you have no fear and push forward, your deeds will win you a victory and you will live. Thus, the route to your safety lies in courageous actions and a keen mind.*

Like every generation, Natori believed that his ancestors were more experienced and skilled in their arts, maybe this was a hearkening back to the "good old days," but for Natori this was an integral part of his belief system. Natori wrote his book in 1681, and as the head of a ninjutsu school, we know his training must have taken place years before that. Take into account that the Edo period under the Tokugawa

*rule started in 1603, and was to become known as the period of peace.
This coincides with the decline of the ninja from their height during
the Warring Period just before 1603. Putting Natori in context, we
see that the people who taught him his ninjutsu would have been either
the older generation who fought as shinobi at the end of the Warring
Period and at the ninja's height of ability, or that he was taught by
someone who was a direct student of a ninja who was at the heart of
the famous Golden Age of the Ninja. The reason for this discussion here
is that Natori explains a play on words that shows us how the ninja
used to be viewed and then how they are viewed in his time. He says
that shinobi are referred to as yato. As Japanese ideograms use both
phonetic and symbolic meanings, this word has two interpretations.
The one that they use in Natori's time is "night-robber" or "thief in the
night." This seems to be the understanding that most people have in
their minds when they think of the ninja. Putting this into historical
context, the ninja had moved away from the strength of their clans
and had started to be used by the government as spies and secret police.
If one takes the other meaning of yato, we see that it can also mean
"night-leader" or "head leader during the night." This would mean
that in times of war they used ninjas differently, and that even the
samurai would bow to their leadership during night excursions. This is
an advance in our understanding of the relationship of the practicality
of the ninja and his role in the political climate. But most important of
all is that this qualifies Natori's lessons as truly authentic as we know
he learned his skills from the archetypal shinobi no mono.*

In essence, there is no specific way of speaking prescribed for a shinobi. You should talk according to the situation and take advantage of the opportunities at hand, if any. You should be aware that what you have prepared in advance within your mind may not always work out successfully. This goes without saying about any dangerous situation. However, an unexpected advantage can always come out of any given condition, when the enemy changes his tactics you must be keen enough to find an opening and exploit it. It is possible for you to stumble upon the answer to your aims by chance, this is not luck if your mind is working as sharply as it can—it is a skill.

Basically, the art of the shinobi is an art to be conducted by bushi warriors, therefore it is not akin to theft or those who perform *yato* 夜とう night-thievery. People in ancient times would also name the shinobi's skills as *yato* 夜頭, but they would use the ideograms that meant night-leader. Respect would have been shown to a good shinobi because they acted as guiding lights and they were entrusted with a number people who were given to them under their command and made captains of troops. In a critical situation the leading shinobi would take charge.

If you enter into a dangerous situation and if the occasion arises, you should not value your life over death. Tradition says that life exists within death and death exists within life. Therefore, if your actions risk the losing of your life and you have no fear, you may find a way out of a desperate situation, however, if you try to survive, you may likely lose your life because you are too stressed to see a way out. Most important is your state of mental awareness and that you should not be torn with the issue of life or death any more.[*]

An old verse:

> *"In this brief life, like a cicada's shell, my body has become empty. There is nothing left of me, so there is nothing to fear."*

---

[*] Literally, "both words of life and death have left me" or "I have let go of my words of life and death."

Because you hold on to your ego, you will be unsettled or upset. If you come with a serene mind, you have nothing to fear. Even when you are furious with anger, as long as you are absorbed in the defeat of others, and have the ability to separate your mind from your emotions—all will be well. This could also be considered as *muga no mushin*, the concept of "no ego" and "no mind."

It is futile to wonder, "What can I plan in advance and what can I perceive through reading a situation in an instant?" Again, if you try to name all such cases then it would seem like Buddhist riddles, and again you will be just like a failed path-seeker on his wandering path. When you have reached the state of complete awareness and gained the utmost secret of this shinobi path, it will not matter to you what you think is necessary and what you think is unnecessary.

I must state that ninpo, the way of the ninja, makes its way, running towards a great void. If you ask what ninpo is, the answer is that it has no shape. If ninpo is sought for, it has no heart. Just try to see and realize clearly the way of your own natural mind.

The Way of Departing

離術法

Rijutsuho

This final chapter is the "Holy Grail" for anyone who wishes to follow the path of a true warrior or wants to discipline themselves in the martial arts. Natori must have been a strong character indeed and a fearsome warrior, because he states that formidableness (without a show of arms), perfect timing, a still mind, military accomplishments, and academic achievement are the true way of the shinobi. If you have all of the above you are like a hawk in flight; other lesser birds will be in awe of your prowess as a warrior, and you will have what is called the "dignity of flying birds."

Natori finishes the Shoninki *with a message that is as clear today as it was over the hills in far away Japan. The message is that a good shinobi knows the minds and hearts of men and that if he is worthy as a shinobi no mono, he will have no enemies and that he will know how to protect his family, allowing his bloodline to continue.*

Do not get over involved in things. If you get stuck on a problem and entangled within it, it is because you cannot let go of yourself but are anxious to pursue issues for your own benefit alone. As mentioned previously, you should keep your true mind righteous and stay out of such silly concerns. You have to realize the ultimate reason and secrets and do not be taken aback or startled by anything.

I hereby inform you that those who shamefully or dishonorably fear the enemy will not be able to read his mind.

Those who have good reasoning in mind and know what they are doing can throw away their own ideas, follow the enemy's mind and wait for the opportunity they need—and if it is the right time, take a thorough and appropriate approach to the target.

It cannot be emphasized enough that you should not be rushed into doing things before the correct timing. Once you ruin an opportunity, it cannot be recalled or remedied. In such a situation, it will be more severe, as if your mind was trapped and cannot escape the forest of thorns. There is a technique named *tobutori*[*] *no kurai* 飛鳥の位, this means "the dignity of flying birds." With this method you can make the enemy follow you as you wish but only by fortifying your body and mind. It is like a hawk flying high up in the sky; all the other birds stay lower in fear of this predator. This is all about formidableness without the need for a physical show of strength, to display your sheer power through spirit alone without violence or action, an aura of supremacy.

Another way to look at the shinobi arts is like a fruit dropping from the tree when it is ripe. It is difficult for the fruit to wait even a short while when it is fully ripe and ready to fall. If your actions are premature, then things will be untimely and all will be ruined—and if too late, you will fall behind. This correct timing is what you should understand properly to be able to understand the minds of men.

Suppose you have to face the enemy without armor or weapons, then know that you have to issue forth good speech, and

---

[*] It is possible to read this as both: *tobutori* or *hicho*

also if you can win over the enemy without fail, it is because your mind is working properly to fulfill the purpose. It shows what is called *shinmyoken* 心妙剣, this is the ability to face an enemy and understand, by sensitivity, his mind and intentions and penetrate his intended plan. With the finest of speech you can kill people without a blade or revive them without medicine; all because of the true value of your mind, wits, and speech. When you master this, you can glide on the edge of a sword or run up an icy hill. All these things can be attained because of the dynamics of your mind.

Those who have a mastery of shinobi arts have no enemies in the world. Thus, I hereby declare this is a book for the prosperity of your offspring and family, keeping your bloodline safe for years to come.

This is the end of the *Shoninki*.

Inscription

奥書

The inscription at the end of the Shoninki *was added 62 years after it was written and was penned by Seiryuken Natori Hyozaemon, who was the grandson of Natori Masatake, our author. Again, we are given vital information about the lifestyle of the ninja. We know that in some cases their skills were only passed from father to son in the ancient fashion. However, we see that this member of the Natori clan decides to pass this knowledge on to another person from another family, that person being Watanabe Rokurozaemon. The final and most compelling line of the* Shoninki *is one that quashes media hype and speculation about the ninja and thrusts us back into the mystery and secret darkness of the ninja, the message is this: "Never show it to anybody!"*

The contents of the *Shoninki*, written above, is not necessarily the path that we should develop and maintain. However, our school of the shinobi arts had to be scribed, because people in the world say that the shinobi, as they are called, have bizarre and peculiar skills and knowingly they skillfully deceive people, but here in this text, the shinobi ways of our school were written down. This considered, if you are confronted by someone performing the shinobi arts, you may find it difficult to conceal your own skills. I suppose every aspect of the deepest secrets has been written down here. You should master these skills with due respect. Unless you know the core elements of the shinobi, there is no way for you to defend against the effects of such skills. Therefore, you should keep working on the shinobi arts within yourself, but do not deceive people with your skills.

This *Shoninki* is the pure and supreme secret of the shinobi arts of our school. Though, since the time of our previous master, this book and the arts written within have been inherited exclusively to none but the only one person. Now, upon the keen request of the inheritor (of this transcription). I hereby give all of this, in entirety, to him. You should master it gracefully with due respect. Displaying this manual to anyone without permission is strictly forbidden.

Seiryuken Natori Hyozaemon 青竜軒 名取兵左衛門
The year of 1743 (Kanpo 3) Year of Yin Water Boar 甘 寛保三歳次癸亥年

Lucky day of the second month 二月吉日
This is given to: Watanabe Rokurozaemon 渡辺六郎左衛門

"Defense Against a Ninja"

A 500-Year-Old

Oral Tradition on Ninjutsu

Tenshinsho-den Katori Shinto-Ryu 天真正伝香取神道流, to give it its full name, is one of the oldest sword schools in Japan. Originating in the late fifteenth century and founded by Lord Iizasa Choisai 飯篠長威斎, who was awarded the divine scroll of his school from a god in the shape of a boy. The school derives its name from the Katori Jingu 香取神宮 shrine in Katori, Chiba prefecture, where the founder is now buried. As this is one of the oldest sword schools, with all of its internal sub-schools, to be registered and recognized in Japan, Katori Shinto-Ryu can also claim to be the oldest form of ninjutsu still to be taught today with an unbroken lineage, as no other body has evidence to predate the school's origins. The martial aspects of the sword school are passed down through ancient scrolls and thus have remained unchanged and unbroken. On the reverse side, the school is also home to a 500-year-old oral tradition and teaches its swordsmen the art of ninjutsu with an emphasis on defense against an attacking shinobi: with the spirit of *know your enemy*. It is recorded here for the first time in English for the martial arts world to enjoy and explore, and was taught to Antony Cummins by Otake Risuke in September of 2009.

Otake sensei 大竹利典, the head teacher, was born in Chiba in 1926. In 1942 he entered the sword school to understand courage and to find a path to valor and the strength to fight in the war if called upon.

I

"In our school there is nothing about learning ninjutsu itself and nothing that is recorded within our ancient scrolls. All the knowledge that I have obtained comes from our founder and has been passed down by word of mouth for over 500 years. This is the true way of defending yourself from a ninja."

II

"A *true* samurai wouldn't do ninjutsu, they in turn would hire a shinobi when necessary."

This statement is the one statement that seems controversial. As is known, the author of the Shoninki *was of samurai status and yet entered the history records as being involved with ninjutsu. Otake sensei himself believes that the* ashigaru, *named Tori Sune'emon* 鳥居強右衛門, *was in fact a ninja.*

III

"Every ninja had a speciality, such as taming and training animals in the mountains, hiding in the water, and hiding among trees amongst other things. In the daytime, they would usually work in the fields as farmers and go about their routine as normal."

The word "ninja" is far too simplistic and generic of a term for there to be a correct understanding of the social context in which ninjas were found. When dealing with the Iga 伊賀 *and Koka* 甲賀 *ninja, there is the belief that they were farming communities. The problem comes when we find that people from Iga and Koka are hired out and do indeed train others in the way of ninjutsu. Thus, we can say that the archetypal ninja is a farmer, but we have to understand that the concept of ninja is much broader then was first thought.*

IV

"Those who tame dogs as a skill would ask how urgent the job was when they got an offer or contract. If the job wasn't urgent they could then use their time to tame the said animal by methods such as feeding or befriending the animal. Or if the need was urgent, they could give a female dog to male or a male dog to female. Also, a shinobi would lure a dog out of its area by food and then proceed to beat the animal badly. They did this while applying a selected scent such as whale oil. This was done so that the dog would re-member the scent at night and fear would then grip the dog as it would recall the near death beating it had received at the hands of the ninja. As a result the dog would run away or cower after giving forth a short bark and investigation into a disturbance.

"Only those who know this skill could know that a shinobi might be there and upon hearing such a reaction from a guard dog. A samurai from our school would take up a bow and shoot into the darkness with the hope of hitting the shinobi."

A selection of manuscripts talk about dogs as the enemy of the ninja, and how to deal with them. The Shoninki *and the* Katori Shinto-Ryu *deal out drastic and deadly punishments for guard dogs.*

V

"They also used other animals which people dislike, such as frogs and snakes, to bring on panic. A shinobi would use this distrac-tion to attain his aim. As a member of my school, you must un-derstand this."

Otake sensei embellished upon how a ninja would train in the wilderness with animals of all kinds, learning how to handle animals and utilize them to their own advantage.

VI

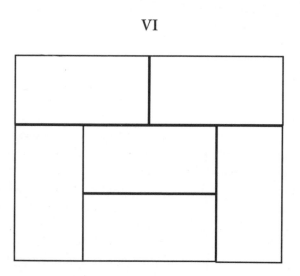

"Tatami mats are laid in the same way for every room that has an external exit. This system of laying down the mats is universal in Japan and nobody can tell you why or how it started. In fact, it started because of the shinobi. You have to remember that in the beginning tatami mats were an expensive commodity and only owned by those of high ranking, thus they were owned by the samurai and were relatively unknown by those who were of lower birth. Where there is a room with a doorway that leads outside you will always find the tatami mats laid out so that you walk across the width of the mat and not so that you walk down its length. The reason for this is simple, tatami mats have their weave in the same way each time and when you lay a mat in this fashion you find that the weave runs in straight lines away from the wall. The shinobi who enters the house of a samurai would automatically use a cross crawl walking style. Thus, as he walked along the wall in this fashion his sideways sliding step would go against the weave of the mat and create a swishing sound that we at this school would be trained to listen for, this is why we lay tatami mats in such a way."

This method of laying mats is called mawashijiki 回り敷き, *where all the mats line the wall. It is said that they are put this way to avoid one mat joining another in front of a doorway but it is impossible to verify if this is indeed the origin for tatami mat plans or if Otake sensei's oral history is correct. However, it is of great interest as it is hard to find a tatami room with an external door that is not laid out in such a way. In reference to the ninja, we can now qualify that they did use the iconic "cross-crawl" stepping action, and as an audience we can now get an understanding of the level of noise that a ninja could not surpass if he wished to avoid detection.*

VII

"The shinobi applied water to the sills of sliding doors so that they wouldn't make noise when stealing in, thus if you find un-explained water around your doors, be warned that a ninja may have entered."

VIII

"When you rush out to chase down shinobi, you shouldn't be barefooted as shinobi scatter caltrops to disable those who are in pursuit."

Caltrops were often dragged behind a ninja, on a piece of rope that the shinobi held in his hand. Throughout all the scrolls, the escape route for a field operative was paramount and it is thought that a ninja would place caltrops at or along this route in preparation for his es-cape. The concept of him simply scattering them around may not be fiction but it is simply not effective. The probability is that some would be placed at specific points while others would be carried on a string in case the ninja was being chased down.

IX

"Those shinobi good at hiding between trees could move around from treetop to treetop as quickly as squirrels. Also, when climbing up a tree, they used their sword as a stepladder or foothold and by lifting themselves up by holding the tree with one arm. They then retrieve their sword by the means of a long cord which they have attached to their weapon. They also climb by swinging a long wet cloth with a snapping action around a branch and ascending from that point."

The image of a ninja using his sword as a foothold and then retrieving it via a long cord is iconic now in the "ninjutsu world" and many references have been made to it. However, Otake sensei here introduces two other techniques. The first was to "hug" the tree with one arm and shimmy up the trunk with his other hand free, presumably for his sword. The second skill was to get a long cloth and soak it in water, then swing the heavy cloth around a branch and let the weight of the wet material wrap around the limb and take hold, thus a ninja could then ascend.

X

"During a night activity, the shinobi would use a bag of charcoal powder from the wood of the *Kiri* tree (*Paulownia*). This wood is very fine in texture and has a distinctive smell. The ninja would apply it to their face and also sprinkle it over and around their body as they moved. Thus, as a defender, you should learn its aroma and then peer into and penetrate the darkness from a low position, close to the ground. If you see something blacker than the darkness moving, be warned—that is a shinobi!"

Surprisingly (or not), this skill is still used today in modern military forces. The art of camouflage is the skill of concealing the human shape. The reason for the standard camouflage pattern of uniforms in the military is to break up the human form, as the eye can recognize this almost immediately. Thus, this black powder used by the ninja would actually break up their shape and make it harder for them to be spotted. Otake sensei then told of how, when you smell this powder, you should take up your bow and shoot randomly into the darkness and into the bushes with the intent of hitting the ninja or scaring them off.

XI

"The image of a ninja hiding in the water with a reed is from manga and is a modern invention. It is ridiculous to contemplate that this works, for even a mosquito will make a ripple on the water, and furthermore a shinobi does not participate in this type of activity in the daytime anyway."

In the Shoninki, *it states that you should use the bamboo pipe to come up for air at intervals so as to not show your face. This skill may have worked in the black of night, but Otake sensei implied that a watchful samurai would be able to spot this without a problem and that this image has been established as a ninja method by modern media. What people often believe is that a ninja will hide in the rushes with this breathing pipe, thereby escaping detection from a passing group. The reality is that a ninja, at night, would swim a body of water and when in need of air, he would come close to the surface, take a breath with his pipe or scabbard and then continue to swim. It was never the act of staying stationary in an attempt to hide.*

XII

"When a shinobi is chased and comes across a pond, they sometimes throw a rock into the water to pretend that they have jumped in. Or they get across the pond by a type of triple long jump, making the pursuers think that they are under the surface. This skill is called *mizugakure* 水隠れ 'hiding in the water.'"

There was confusion here as to the type of jump Otake sensei is describing, the closest translation that can be identified is that of a triple long jump. Upon questioning Otake sensei on this technique, we came to a wall in the description of its execution. It appears to have been a jumping skill that gets the ninja to the other side of the small river while also making the sound of a person entering the water, thus having the effect of the people giving chase believing that the ninja is in the water, whereas in reality he is in hiding on the other bank.

XIII

Was Torii Sune'emon a Ninja?

"There was a foot soldier called Torii Sune'emon who I think was a ninja performing the art of *mizugakure*. It is said that he swam a river, infiltrating enemy territory for over 3.5 miles (6 km) without being noticed and then he ran more than 18 miles (30 km), even though he had to escape from his fortress, which was besieged by the Takeda's force of over 15,000 men. The river was said to be booby-trapped and under heavy security. To me it seems like this man was more than likely a ninja."

It is unknown here if Otake sensei has this opinion from his own research or whether this is information passed down to him. Either way, it does seem like a classic shinobi activity, and in such circumstances it is probable that a ninja would be called upon. However, from a historian's point of view this is only speculation.

XIV

"When caught within a prison, shinobi soldiers can communicate with each other by imitating the sound of birds such as water rails, or crickets. This skill is called *kuina onkyo* クイナ音響. When they do this they lie down and bring their mouth and ears close to the floor. If you hear these sounds while you have a captured ninja, be warned that they may be communicating in this way. Also, with this skill, a ninja could place his ear to the ground and hear cavalry moving 500–1,000 feet away (about 200–300 meters), determining their number and the direction in which they were heading."

As inconceivable as this sounds, we can gain an understanding that the ninja did use an instrument for listening to the ground and detecting enemy movement, we know this from a few sources. However, the distance that they could hear is still lost to us without experimentation.

XV

"When a shinobi aims to steal documents or something of the like, they sometimes achieve this by taking two mice with them on a mission. They steal into the house when everyone has fallen asleep and let a single mouse go to create a fuss. After the people have settled back down and asleep, again the shinobi lets the second mouse enter. This makes the household think that there is an infestation of mice and the house awakens to deal with the problem. During this confusion, the shinobi can steal what he wants without effort. This is one way of taming animals, a swordsman of my school should understand this trick."

The author discussed this point with Nakashima sensei, who fully supports the idea of ninja using animals as part of their arsenal. There are several accounts within the scrolls of using animals for misdirection. Nakashima sensei also went on to describe that a shinobi would use this trick to get the occupants to leave a given room, as they would almost certainly leave the room to find the source of the infestation.

XVI

"When you think you are being pursued by a shinobi or someone of ill intent, you should walk in the middle of the road so that you will not be stabbed from behind the bushes while you walk along them."

At points, Otake sensei's information correlates to the historical documents with amazing accuracy. The Shoninki *states that as ninja should walk along the edges of bushes as to imitate a dog's behavior and thus you can follow a target or evade a passer-by. Therefore, this is a perfect defense against a ninja technique.*

XVII

"When you stay at an inn, you shouldn't sleep on a futon that has been prepared for you. The staff may have been bribed and may have given over information as to where you are sleeping to a shinobi. You should move your futon without being noticed so that a ninja will be misled."

Again, this coincides dramatically with the historical literature, it is said that a shinobi should bribe local people for information that they need and also, in the Shoninki, *it instructs the ninja on how to get information of this kind from a conversation without your opponent knowing your intentions.*

XVIII

"Those in the ancient times used wolves' droppings to make smoke signals as the droppings of wolves make very good smoke, a smoke which will resist the wind and go straight and high in the sky.

"When in the woods and confronted by wolves you should hold a stick above your head, vertical and high. A wolf will not attack anything that it cannot jump over, thus hold the stick high and the wolf will not attack.

"A story that has been passed down to me is as follows: Wolves once put out the fire that woodsmen left alight within the woods. The wolf pack ran down to the river, submerged themselves and then went back to the fire and doused the flames."

The first quote is directly related to ninjutsu as wolf dropping smoke signals are mentioned elsewhere within the records. The second two Otake sensei ascribes to "ancient woodsmen's knowledge" that has been passed down to him through his school.

XIX

"When you get lost in the mountains and come across a cross-road, you should taste the soil, for the road which people walk along will taste salty and you can discern the most traveled route.

"When lost in the mountains, descend to find a river, follow that river down hill and you will find a village along it."

Remembering that "roads" in medieval Japan, especially in the mountains where it's more likely to be a "path," it would seem plausible that a well-traveled road may have a higher salt content from human sweat. However, this would have to be tested, but this statement appears in more than one account.

XX

"Shinobi swords have leather handguards instead of iron. This is so that they will not rattle when moving around, they also have shorter blades and a longer cord."

This is an obvious step for a shinobi to take and highly plausible, the need for a silenced sword is also repeated in the other manuscripts. Also, the Shoninki *states that* an o-wakizashi 大脇差 *is best, which is, of course, a short sword.*

XXI

"*Kuji-in* 九字印 and *kuji-kiri* 九字切 are for self-concentration and to be used as a magical power. The spells themselves come from Sanskrit and their meanings are not understood. *Juji* 十字, or 'ten signs' contains an ideogram within the *kuji* grid of nine lines. For example, you write the kanji for 'dragon' in the *kuji* grid and when you are going to board a ship, you use a dragon as the tenth symbol, as for us, the dragon is the lord of the water. We, as swordsmen of this school, use the spells and the *juji* to protect ourselves from the shinobi, have faith and believe, for it truly works!"

Kuji is an expansive field with countless debates surrounding it. The basic principle is that kuji *is split into two sections. The first is named* kuji-in *and is a selection of nine hand positions that are accompanied by a mantra and a specific direction of concentration. The second is the* kuji-kiri, *this is the concept of cutting nine lines in the air and creating a grid. From here you draw the tenth sign, which is a kanji character that the adept feels is correct for the situation, as described above. The first use of* kuji *is for empowerment and concentration, the second is ritualistic magic. The origins of* kuji *date back to Hinduism and are not, as commonly believed, used by the ninja alone.*

XXII

"*Kozuka* 小柄 are the small blades found next to the hilt of a katana, these are often portrayed as being used as shuriken by the ninja. This is also not true, they were expensive and hard to replace, and thus their real use was for cooking and peeling vegetables, nothing quite as exciting as a shuriken."

The image of a ninja agent incognito, throwing these small side knives from the hilt of a katana is rife within the ninja media, but this is a media created image. It is within reason that a person would use this knife for combat if the situation dictated it. However, to throw them as shuriken would indeed become an expensive venture.

XXIII

"I am the master of this school, but even when I throw straight shuriken I cannot become accurate at more than a room's length, so do not believe some of the mystical abilities some people attribute to shuriken masters."

A balance has to be reached here between what is expected of a shuriken master and what is reality. To the average person, a master shuriken thrower may be able to perform amazing feats, but to a master of shuriken-jutsu, the fabled arts of the ninja can become outra-

geous. As we observe the martial and historical world, we can postulate that a circus knife thrower would have a similar ability as a shuriken master of the past, thus, fitting this template onto our historical ninja, we can refine our concept of the accurate range of the shuriken.

XXIV

"About *yo-nin* 陽忍 and *in-nin* 陰忍:

To infiltrate a mansion or somewhere else, a shinobi used two methods: *Yo-nin*, the method by which you perform the skills by revealing yourself in the daytime, and secondly, *in-nin*, the method by which you perform infiltration skills without showing yourself at night."

This is an important element when investigating ninjutsu. Many people do not understand the difference here, or at least they argue that a ninja would only do one of these methods. In or yin, *is the female and darker side of the "balance" and constitutes what we could call the classic ninja methods. While* yo *or* yang *methods are the light and open sides of ninjutsu, the method of being in plain sight, yet unnoticed by the world. Both In-nin and Yo-nin are words that have not been used within the modern "ninjutsu" community, which is extraordinary as they form the fundamental core of the shinobi arts.*

XXV

"A shinobi could utilize the advantages of the three major elements, they are of Heaven, Earth, and Man 天地人. An example of Heaven 天 (astronomy) is to choose a moonless night and apply the charcoal powder of the *Kiri* tree to remain unnoticed by the enemy. An example of Earth 地 (topography) is to climb a tree by using a sword or cloth and to use the nature of the earth to your advantage. An example of Man 人 (psychology) is captured in an anecdote handed down through my school and is as follows:

'There was a very smart young man and two old men. One day, the old men decided to test how good the young man really was.

They invited him to their home and gave him alcohol saying, "We have hidden a wallet somewhere on this property as a test for you today. Can you tell where it is?" In a few minutes, he answered its exact position, which was in the garden around the back of the stone lantern. He knew that because he had guessed their intentions beforehand as the invitation was not so natural and he noticed they were casting glances in that direction.'

"This is the way of 'Man' in ninjutsu."

The three-point system of "Heaven, Earth, and Man" are known in some ninjutsu research circles, but generally they are not well known. This trinity also appears in other sections of Eastern culture and can be seen as an attempt by the ninja to understand the world around them and the ways it can be manipulated.

XXVI

"A shinobi had such good strength and skills that he could run over 60 miles (more than 95 km) without drinking or eating anything. When tired, they would dig a 1 foot (30 cm) ditch, where the soil is not firm and rest by lying within it, taking deep breaths for a short while. It revived them so that they could run dozens of kilometers again. In ancient times it was said that tremendous energy can be found in the ground, and the shinobi utilized it."

This highlights a quality that has been long forgotten and for which the ninja were originally famous, and that was their amazing endurance. To run 60 miles in a day is by no means an unbelievable feat, especially for the ancient world. Modern athletes run double marathons, and military forces can come close to that amount. Thus, this is a legitimate skill that is attainable depending on one's level of fitness.

XXVII

"When a shinobi ran a long distance, they employed a unique running method. They would take big steps on one leg and natural steps on the other leg. When the leg which is taking the larger steps becomes tired, they simply changed legs."

Oral Traditions Not Related to Ninjutsu:

XXVIII

"In our school, there is a rule that we should not serve as a swordsman for any warlords, no matter how much of a stipend they offer. This is because if a master orders you to kill, even a friend or a family member, you cannot refuse them. It would be difficult for you to respect both your honor and loyalty under such a contract. Thus, even though many famous warriors came to have a match or to be trained at our school, none of them appear in fictional literature."

The school still asks students to sign an enrollment paper in their own blood. A prospective student must promise to stick to a selection of rules, in which the above stipulation is included.

XXIX

"Our school's founding master was Iizasa Ienao 飯篠家直 and he became enlightened after three years of praying at the Katori shrine. He taught that the art of war is the art of peace, where defeating the enemy without fighting is better than defeating him by force of arms."

XXX

"Once, a samurai came to have a match with Ienao, our founder. So, Ienao put a thin mat over dwarf bamboo sections and sat on it without effort or without destroying the elevated and fragile seat. He then told the opponent to do the same and he would have a match after they had talked, but the samurai couldn't repeat that feat and ended up becoming a disciple of his. The original master was always moving along the path of perfection by learning tantric Buddhism as well as Shinto. He tried to find the way of peace."

XXXI

"In this picture of my founding master, he looks so relaxed but yet he has no gaps from where to get in and attack. I used to have this picture in my bedroom and I prayed to him daily, I prayed that I would be as close as possible to his level some day. However, one morning I had a vision that the master hit me with his shuriken so quickly; he simply threw it from the posture you see him in now. I then moved the picture into the next room where it stays."

At the interview, Otake sensei described how he would sit before the image each day and pray. As can be seen by the picture, the "ba-

ton" being held is held from the top with the point on the floor. Otake sensei states that in this vision, the figure did not prepare his shuriken by lifting his hand, he simply shot from this posture and startled the school master.

XXXII
About the skill of *atemi* 当て身 slapping:

"A skill we teach in our school is that of Atemi. It can deliver serious damage, even a woman can do serious injury to a man. It's most effective when done on the *jinchu* 人中 point (between the nose and the lips), on the stomach, the bottom of the spine or other pressure points. A hit to the eyes could damage the enemy's eyesight for up to ten days."

Bibliography

正忍記，全三巻，藤一水子正武，国立国会図書館蔵本
忍術伝書　正忍記　藤一水子正武　著　中島篤巳　解読・
解説　新人物往来社
甦った忍術伝書　正忍記，木村山治郎，　紀尾井書房
南紀徳川史第六冊，巻之五十九
和歌山県史　人物，　和歌山県史編さん委員会
武芸流派大事典，　綿谷雪　山田忠史共編，　新人物往来社
万川集海，　藤林保武，　国立公文書館所蔵
忍秘伝，　沖森直三郎編，　沖森書店
太平記　日本古典文学大系34，後藤丹治　釜田喜三郎　校
注，岩波書店
義経記　日本古典文学大系37，岡見正雄　校注，岩波書店
平家物語　新日本古典文学大系，梶原正昭・山下宏明　校
注，岩波書店
萬川集海　陽忍篇，　監修　石田善人，　訳柚木俊一郎，
誠秀堂
忍術秘伝の書，中島篤巳　著，角川書店
概説　忍者・忍術，　山北篤　著，新紀元社

図説　忍者と忍術，歴史群像シリーズ，学研
忍びの者132人データファイル，　別冊歴史読本，新人物
往来社
禅と日本文化，鈴木大拙　著，北川桃雄　訳，岩波新書
走る悪党，蜂起する土民（全集　日本の歴史7）　小学館
日本史モノ事典，㈱平凡社
続日本史モノ事典，㈱平凡社
江戸城御庭番―徳川将軍の耳と目　中公新書，深井雅海，
中央公論社
忍術　その歴史と忍者，　奥瀬平七郎，新人物往来社
忍者と忍術　中公文庫，戸部新十郎，中央公論社
史談太平記の超人たち―後醍醐天皇・正成・尊氏，上田
滋，中央公論新社
陰陽道とは何か―日本史を呪縛する神秘の原理　PHP新
書，戸矢学，PHP研究所

About the Author

Antony Cummins heads the Historical Ninjutsu Research Team, a project that documents, translates and publishes medieval documents pertaining to the shinobi of Japan. Alongside this, Antony has revived an old samurai school of war, Natori-Ryu, with the aim of educating people on historical Japanese warfare. His aim is to establish a correct understanding of Japanese military arts and to bring about a deeper understanding and respect for Japanese arts. He is on most social media platforms, and information can be found at www.natori.co.uk.

Also by the Author
Books

Samurai and Ninja
Book of Samurai
Book of Ninja
Iga and Koka Ninja Skills
Secret Traditions of the Shinobi
Samurai War Stories
In Search of the Ninja

About the Translator

Yoshie Minami was born in Tokyo and currently lives in Saitama, Japan. She has a B.A. degree in Linguistics from the International Christian University. As a translator, she has a published イギリス英語の悪口雑言辞典 *True English* (東京堂出版—2009).